PENGUIN TWENTIETH-CENTURY CLASSICS

COMPLETE POEMS

Marianne Moore was born in Kirkwood, Missouri, on November 15, 1887, and spent much of her youth in Carlisle, Pennsylvania. After graduation from Bryn Mawr College in 1909 she taught for four years at the Carlisle Indian School. Her poetry first appeared professionally in *The Egoist* and *Poetry* magazines in 1915, and she moved to New York City in 1918. Her first book, *Poems*, was issued in England by the Egoist Press in 1921. *Observations*, published three years later in America, received the Dial Award. From 1925 to 1929 she served as acting editor of *The Dial*, the preeminent American literary periodical. She moved to Brooklyn in 1929, where she lived for the next thirty-six years. In 1935 *Selected Poems*, with an Introduction by T. S. Eliot, brought her work to the attention of a wider public.

Three additional books of poetry were followed, in 1951, by her *Collected Poems*, which won the Bollingen Prize, the National Book Award, and the Pulitzer Prize. She went on to publish a verse translation of the complete *Fables of La Fontaine*, a collection of critical essays, and three more volumes of poems.

Among the many awards Marianne Moore received are the National Institute of Arts and Letters Gold Medal for Poetry, the Poetry Society of America's Gold Medal for Distinguished Achievement, and the National Medal for Literature, America's highest literary honor. A member of the National Institute of Arts and Letters since 1947, she was elected to the American Academy of Arts and Letters in 1955. In 1967 she was made Chevalier de l'Ordre des Arts et des Lettres by the French Republic, and in 1969 she received an hononary doctorate in literature from Harvard University, her sixteenth hononary degree. Marianne More died in New York City, in her eighty-fifth year, on February 5, 1972.

COMPLETE POEMS

MARIANNE MOORE

MACMILLIAN PUBLISHING CO., INC
PENGUIN BOOKS

PENGUIN BOOKS

Published by the Penguin Group

Penguin Group (USA) Inc., 375 Hudson Street, New York, New York 10014, U.S.A.

Penguin Books Ltd, 80 Strand, London WC2R ORL, England

Penguin Books Australia Ltd, 250 Camberwell Road, Camberwell, Victoria 3124, Australia

Penguin Books Canada Ltd, 10 Alcorn Avenue, Toronto, Ontario, Canada M4V 3B2

Penguin Books India (P) Ltd, 11 Community Centre, Panchsheel Park, New Delhi – 110 017, India

Penguin Group (NZ), cnr Airborne and Rosedale Roads, Albany, Auckland 1310, New Zealand

Penguin Books (South Africa) (Pty) Ltd, 24 Sturdee Avenue,

Rosebank, Johannesburg 2196, South Africa

Penguin Books Ltd, Registered Offices: 80 Strand, London WC2R ORL, England

First published in the United States of America by
The Macmillan Company and The Viking Press 1967
This edition first published by Macmillan Publishing Co., Inc.,
and The Viking Press 1981
Published by Macmillan Publishing Co., Inc., and Penguin Books 1982
This edition published by Macmillan Publishing Company/Penguin Books 1994

20

Certain of these poems first appeared in *Active Anthology, Art News, Art News Annual, Atlantic Monthly, Boston Sun Globe, Botteghe Oscure, Broom*, Bryn Mawr College (*The Lantern, Tipyn O'Bob, The Title*), *Chimera, City Center Souvenir Program 1962* (New York), *Contemporary Poetry, Contemporary Verse, The Criterion, Decision, The Dial, The Egoist, Furioso, Harper's Bazaar, Harvard Advocate, Horizon, Hound and Horn, Imagi, Kenyon Review, Ladies' Home Journal, Life and Letters Today, The Listener, The Nation, New Directions, New English Weekly, The New Republic, New York Herald Tribune, Others, Others Anthology 1917, Partisan Review*, Perspectives U S A, *Poetry, Poetry in Crystal, Quarterly Review of Literature, Literary Supplement* (London), *Virginia Quarterly Review, Vogue*, and *What's New.*

Twenty-three of the poems in this edition appeared originally in *The New Yorker.*

LIBRARY OF CONGRESS CATALOGUING IN PUBLICATION DATA
Moore, Marianne, 1887–1972.
The complete poems of Marianne Moore.
Includes index.
ISBN 0 14 01.8851 7
I. Title.
PS3525.05616A17   1981   811'.52   82–6608   AACR2

Printed in the United States of America
Set in Monotype Waldbaum

Omissions are not accidents.

M.M.

A NOTE ON THE TEXT

The text conforms as closely as is now possible to the author's final intentions. Five of the poems written after the first printing of this volume have been included. Late authorized corrections, and earlier corrections authorized but not made, have been incorporated. Punctuation, hyphens, and line arrangements silently changed by editor, proofreader, or typesetter have been restored. Misleading editorial amplifications of the notes have been removed.

Clive Driver

Contents

WHAT ARE YEARS (1941)

II. LATER POEMS

LIKE A BULWARK (1956)

O TO BE A DRAGON (1959)

TELL ME, TELL ME (1966)

HITHERTO UNCOLLECTED

Selections *from* THE FABLES OF LA FONTAINE (1954)

. Collected Poems (1951)

TO MARY WARNER MOORE (1862–1947)

SELECTED POEMS (1935)

THE STEEPLE-JACK

Dürer would have seen a reason for living
    in a town like this, with eight stranded whales
to look at; with the sweet sea air coming into your house
on a fine day, from water etched
    with waves as formal as the scales
on a fish.

One by one in two's and three's, the seagulls keep
    flying back and forth over the town clock,
or sailing around the lighthouse without moving their wings—
rising steadily with a slight
    quiver of the body—or flock
mewing where

a sea the purple of the peacock's neck is
    paled to greenish azure as Dürer changed
the pine green of the Tyrol to peacock blue and guinea
gray. You can see a twenty-five-
    pound lobster; and fish nets arranged
to dry. The

whirlwind fife-and-drum of the storm bends the salt
    marsh grass, disturbs stars in the sky and the
star on the steeple; it is a privilege to see so
much confusion. Disguised by what
    might seem the opposite, the sea-
side flowers and

trees are favored by the fog so that you have
    the tropics at first hand: the trumpet-vine,
fox-glove, giant snap-dragon, a salpiglossis that has

spots and stripes; morning-glories, gourds,
    or moon-vines trained on fishing-twine
at the back door;

cat-tails, flags, blueberries and spiderwort,
    striped grass, lichens, sunflowers, asters, daisies—
yellow and crab-claw ragged sailors with green bracts—toad-plant,
petunias, ferns; pink lilies, blue
    ones, tigers; poppies; black sweet-peas.
The climate

is not right for the banyan, frangipani, or
    jack-fruit trees; or for exotic serpent
life. Ring lizard and snake-skin for the foot, if you see fit;
but here they've cats, not cobras, to
    keep down the rats. The diffident
little newt

with white pin-dots on black horizontal spaced-
    out bands lives here; yet there is nothing that
ambition can buy or take away. The college student
named Ambrose sits on the hillside
    with his not-native books and hat
and sees boats

at sea progress white and rigid as if in
    a groove. Liking an elegance of which
the source is not bravado, he knows by heart the antique
sugar-bowl shaped summer-house of
    interlacing slats, and the pitch
of the church

spire, not true, from which a man in scarlet lets
    down a rope as a spider spins a thread;
he might be part of a novel, but on the sidewalk a
sign says C. J. Poole, Steeple-Jack,

in black and white; and one in red
and white says

Danger. The church portico has four fluted
        columns, each a single piece of stone, made
modester by white-wash. This would be a fit haven for
waifs, children, animals, prisoners,
        and presidents who have repaid
sin-driven

senators by not thinking about them. The
        place has a school-house, a post-office in a
store, fish-houses, hen-houses, a three-masted
        schooner on
the stocks. The hero, the student,
        the steeple-jack, each in his way,
is at home.

It could not be dangerous to be living
        in a town like this, of simple people,
who have a steeple-jack placing danger-signs by the church
while he is gilding the solid-
        pointed star, which on a steeple
stands for hope.

THE HERO

Where there is personal liking we go.
   Where the ground is sour; where there are
   weeds of beanstalk height,
   snakes' hypodermic teeth, or
   the wind brings the "scarebabe voice"
   from the neglected yew set with
   the semi-precious cat's eyes of the owl—
awake, asleep, "raised ears extended to fine points," and so
on—love won't grow.

We do not like some things, and the hero
   doesn't; deviating head-stones
   and uncertainty;
   going where one does not wish
   to go; suffering and not
   saying so; standing and listening where something
   is hiding. The hero shrinks
as what it is flies out on muffled wings, with twin yellow
eyes—to and fro—

with quavering water-whistle note, low,
   high, in basso-falsetto chirps
   until the skin creeps.
   Jacob when a-dying, asked
   Joseph: Who are these? and blessed
   both sons, the younger most, vexing Joseph. And
   Joseph was vexing to some.
Cincinnatus was; Regulus; and some of our fellow
men have been, although devout,

like Pilgrim having to go slow
   to find his roll; tired but hopeful—
   hope not being hope

until all ground for hope has
vanished; and lenient, looking
upon a fellow creature's error with the
feelings of a mother—a
woman or a cat. The decorous frock-coated Negro
by the grotto

answers the fearless sightseeing hobo
who asks the man she's with, what's this,
what's that, where's Martha
buried, "Gen-ral Washington
there; his lady, here"; speaking
as if in a play—not seeing her; with a
sense of human dignity
and reverence for mystery, standing like the shadow
of the willow.

Moses would not be grandson to Pharaoh.
It is not what I eat that is
my natural meat,
the hero says. He's not out
seeing a sight but the rock
crystal thing to see—the startling El Greco
brimming with inner light—that
covets nothing that it has let go. This then you may know
as the hero.

THE JERBOA

Too Much

A Roman had an
artist, a freedman,
   contrive a cone—pine-cone
   or fir-cone—with holes for a fountain. Placed on
     the Prison of St. Angelo, this cone
     of the Pompeys which is known

now as the Popes', passed
for art. A huge cast
   bronze, dwarfing the peacock
   statue in the garden of the Vatican,
     it looks like a work of art made to give
     to a Pompey, or native

of Thebes. Others could
build, and understood
   making colossi and
   how to use slaves, and kept crocodiles and put
     baboons on the necks of giraffes to pick
     fruit, and used serpent magic.

They had their men tie
hippopotami
   and bring out dappled dog-
   cats to course antelopes, dikdik, and ibex;
     or used small eagles. They looked on as theirs,
     impalas and onigers,

the wild ostrich herd
with hard feet and bird
   necks rearing back in the

dust like a serpent preparing to strike, cranes,
    mongooses, storks, anoas, Nile geese;
    and there were gardens for these—

combining planes, dates,
limes, and pomegranates,
    in avenues—with square
    pools of pink flowers, tame fish, and small frogs. Besides
        yarns dyed with indigo, and red cotton,
        they had a flax which they spun

into fine linen
cordage for yachtsmen.
    These people liked small things;
    they gave to boys little paired playthings such as
        nests of eggs, ichneumon and snake, paddle
        and raft, badger and camel;

and made toys for them-
selves: the royal totem;
    and toilet-boxes marked
    with the contents. Lords and ladies put goose-grease
        paint in round bone boxes—the pivoting
        lid incised with a duck-wing

or reverted duck-
head; kept in a buck
    or rhinoceros horn,
    the ground horn; and locust oil in stone locusts.
        It was a picture with a fine distance;
        of drought, and of assistance

in time, from the Nile
rising slowly, while
    the pig-tailed monkey on
    slab-hands, with arched-up slack-slung gait, and the brown

dandy looked at the jasmine two-leafed twig
and bud, cactus-pads, and fig.

Dwarfs here and there, lent
to an evident
   poetry of frog grays,
    duck-egg greens, and egg-plant blues, a fantasy
     and a verisimilitude that were
     right to those with, everywhere,

power over the poor.
The bees' food is your
   food. Those who tended flower-
    beds and stables were like the king's cane in the
     form of a hand, or the folding bedroom
     made for his mother of whom

he was fond. Princes
clad in queens' dresses,
   calla or petunia
    white, that trembled at the edge, and queens in a
     king's underskirt of fine-twilled thread like silk-
     worm gut, as bee-man and milk-

maid, kept divine cows
and bees; limestone brows,
   and gold-foil wings. They made
    basalt serpents and portraits of beetles; the
     king gave his name to them and he was named
     for them. He feared snakes, and tamed

Pharaoh's rat, the rust-
backed mongoose. No bust
   of it was made, but there
    was pleasure for the rat. Its restlessness was

its excellence; it was praised for its wit;
and the jerboa, like it,

a small desert rat,
and not famous, that
   lives without water, has
      happiness. Abroad seeking food, or at home
         in its burrow, the Sahara field-mouse
            has a shining silver house

of sand. O rest and
joy, the boundless sand,
   the stupendous sand-spout,
      no water, no palm-trees, no ivory bed,
         tiny cactus; but one would not be he
            who has nothing but plenty.

Abundance

Africanus meant
the conqueror sent
   from Rome. It should mean the
      untouched: the sand-brown jumping-rat—free-born; and
         the blacks, that choice race with an elegance
            ignored by one's ignorance.

Part terrestrial,
and part celestial,
   Jacob saw, cudgel staff
      in claw-hand—steps of air and air angels; his
         friends were the stones. The translucent mistake
            of the desert, does not make

hardship for one who
can rest and then do

the opposite—launching
as if on wings, from its match-thin hind legs, in
    daytime or at night; with the tail as a weight,
    undulated out by speed, straight.

Looked at by daylight,
the underside's white,
    though the fur on the back
    is buff-brown like the breast of the fawn-breasted
        bower-bird. It hops like the fawn-breast, but has
        chipmunk contours—perceived as

it turns its bird head—
the nap directed
    neatly back and blending
    with the ear which reiterates the slimness
        of the body. The fine hairs on the tail,
        repeating the other pale

markings, lengthen until
at the tip they fill
    out in a tuft—black and
    white; strange detail of the simplified creature,
        fish-shaped and silvered to steel by the force
        of the large desert moon. Course

the jerboa, or
plunder its food store,
    and you will be cursed. It
    honors the sand by assuming its color;
        closed upper paws seeming one with the fur
        in its flight from a danger.

By fifths and sevenths,
in leaps of two lengths,
    like the uneven notes

of the Bedouin flute, it stops its gleaning
    on little wheel castors, and makes fern-seed
    foot-prints with kangaroo speed.

Its leaps should be set
to the flageolet;
    pillar body erect
on a three-cornered smooth-working Chippendale
    claw—propped on hind legs, and tail as third toe,
    between leaps to its burrow.

CAMELLIA SABINA

and the Bordeaux plum
from Marmande (France) in parenthesis with
A.G. on the base of the jar—Alexis Godillot—
unevenly blown beside a bubble that
is green when held up to the light; they
are a fine duet; the screw-top
    for this graft-grown briar-black bloom
on black-thorn pigeon's-blood,
    is, like Certosa, sealed with foil. Appropriate custom.

And they keep under
glass also, camellias catalogued by
lines across the leaf. The French are a cruel race—willing
to squeeze the diner's cucumber or broil a
meal on vine-shoots. Gloria mundi
with a leaf two inches, nine lines
    broad, they have; and the smaller,
Camellia Sabina
    with amanita-white petals; there are several of her

pale pinwheels, and pale
stripe that looks as if on a mushroom the
sliver from a beet-root carved into a rose were laid. "Dry
the windows with a cloth fastened to a staff.
In the camellia-house there must be
no smoke from the stove, or dew on
    the windows, lest the plants ail,"
the amateur is told;
    "mistakes are irreparable and nothing will avail."

A scentless nosegay
is thus formed in the midst of the bouquet

from bottles, casks and corks, for sixty-four million red wines
and twenty million white, which Bordeaux merchants
and lawyers "have spent a great deal of
trouble" to select, from what was
and what was not Bordeaux. A
food-grape, however—"born
of nature and of art"—is true ground for the grape-holiday.

The food of a wild
mouse in some countries is wild parsnip- or sunflower- or
morning-glory-seed, with an occasional
grape. Underneath the vines of the Bolzano
grape of Italy, the Prince of Tails
might stroll. Does yonder mouse with a
grape in its hand and its child
in its mouth, not portray
the Spanish fleece suspended by the neck? In that well-piled

larder above your
head, the picture of what you will eat is
looked at from the end of the avenue. The wire cage is
locked, but by bending down and studying the
roof, it is possible to see the
pantomime of Persian thought: the
gilded, too tight undemure
coat of gems unruined
by the rain—each small pebble of jade that refused to mature,

plucked delicately
off. Off jewelry not meant to keep Tom
Thumb, the cavalry cadet, on his Italian upland
meadow-mouse, from looking at the grapes beneath
the interrupted light from them, and
dashing round the *concours hippique*
of the tent, in a flurry

of eels, scallops, serpents,
   and other shadows from the blue of the green canopy.

   The wine-cellar? No.
It accomplishes nothing and makes the
soul heavy. The gleaning is more than the vintage, though the
history *de la Vigne et du vin* has placed
mirabelle in the *bibliothèque*
unique depuis seventeen-ninety-seven.
   (Close the window,
says the Abbé Berlèse,
   for Sabina born under glass.) O generous Bolzano!

NO SWAN SO FINE

"No water so still as the
    dead fountains of Versailles." No swan,
with swart blind look askance
and gondoliering legs, so fine
    as the chintz china one with fawn-
brown eyes and toothed gold
collar on to show whose bird it was.

Lodged in the Louis Fifteenth
    candelabrum-tree of cockscomb-
tinted buttons, dahlias,
sea-urchins, and everlastings,
    it perches on the branching foam
of polished sculptured
flowers—at ease and tall. The king is dead.

THE PLUMET BASILISK

In Costa Rica

In blazing driftwood
   the green keeps showing at the same place;
as, intermittently, the fire-opal shows blue and green.
   In Costa Rica the true Chinese lizard face
is found, of the amphibious falling dragon, the living fire-work.

He leaps and meets his
   likeness in the stream and, king with king,
helped by his three-part plume along the back, runs on two legs,
   tail dragging; faints upon the air; then with a spring
dives to the stream-bed, hiding as the chieftain with gold body
                                hid in

Guatavita Lake.
   He runs, he flies, he swims, to get to
his basilica—"the ruler of Rivers, Lakes, and Seas,
   invisible or visible," with clouds to do
as bid—and can be "long or short, and also coarse or fine at
                                   pleasure."

The Malay Dragon

We have ours; and they
   have theirs. Ours has a skin feather crest;
theirs has wings out from the waist which is snuff-brown or sallow.
   Ours falls from trees on water; theirs is the smallest
dragon that knows how to dive head-first from a tree-top to some-
                                   thing dry.

Floating on spread ribs,
   the boat-like body settles on the

clamshell-tinted spray sprung from the nut·meg tree—minute legs
    trailing half akimbo—the true divinity
of Malay. Among unfragrant orchids, on the unnutritious nut-

tree, *myristica*
    fragrans, the harmless god spreads ribs that
do not raise a hood. This is the serpent-dove peculiar
    to the East; that lives as the butterfly or bat
can, in a brood, conferring wings on what it grasps, as the air-plant
                         does.

The Tuatera

Elsewhere, sea lizards—
    congregated so there is not room
to step, with tails laid criss-cross, alligator-style, among
    birds toddling in and out—are innocent of whom
they neighbor. Bird-reptile social life is pleasing. The tuatera

will tolerate a
    petrel in its den, and lays ten eggs
or nine—the number laid by dragons since "a true dragon
    has nine sons." The frilled lizard, the kind with no legs,
and the three-horned chameleon, are non-serious ones that take
                    to flight
if you do not. In
    Copenhagen the principal door
of the bourse is roofed by two pairs of dragons standing on
    their heads—twirled by the architect—so that the four
green tails conspiring upright, symbolize four-fold security.

In Costa Rica

Now, where sapotans drop
    their nuts out on the stream, there is, as

I have said, one of the quickest lizards in the world—the
  basilisk—that feeds on leaves and berries and has
shade from palm-vines, ferns, and peperomias; or lies basking on a

horizontal branch
  from which sour-grass and orchids sprout. If
beset, he lets go, smites the water, and runs on it—a thing
  difficult for fingered feet. But when captured—stiff
and somewhat heavy, like fresh putty on the hand—he is no longer

the slight lizard that
  can stand in a receding flattened
S—small, long and vertically serpentine or, sagging,
  span the bushes in a fox's bridge. Vines suspend
the weight of his faint shadow fixed on silk.

As by a Chinese brush, eight green
bands are painted on
  the tail—as piano keys are barred
by five black stripes across the white. This octave of faulty
  decorum hides the extraordinary lizard
till night-fall, which is for man the basilisk whose look will kill;
                                                                but is

for lizards men can
  kill, the welcome dark—with galloped
ground-bass of the military drum, the squeak of bag-pipes
  and of bats. Hollow whistled monkey-notes disrupt
the castanets. Taps from the back of the bow sound odd on last
                                                      year's gourd,

or when they touch the
  kettledrums—at which (for there's no light),
a scared frog, screaming like a bird, leaps out from weeds in which
  it could have hid, with curves of the meteorite,

wide water-bug strokes,
in jerks which express
a regal and excellent awkwardness,

    the basilisk portrays
mythology's wish
to be interchangeably man and fish—

traveling rapidly upward, as
spider-clawed fingers can twang the
bass strings of the harp, and with steps
as articulate, make their way
back to retirement on strings that
vibrate till the claws are spread flat.

    Among tightened wires,
minute noises swell
and change, as in the woods' acoustic shell

they will with trees as avenues of steel to veil

as from black opal emerald opal emerald—
scale which Swinburne called in prose, the
noiseless music that hangs about
the serpent when it stirs or springs.

No anonymous
    nightingale sings in a swamp, fed on
sound from porcupine-quilled palm-trees
    that rattle like the rain. This is our Tower-of-London
jewel that the Spaniards failed to see, among the feather capes

and hawk's-head moths and black-chinned
    humming-birds; the innocent, rare, gold-

defending dragon that as you look begins to be a
   nervous naked sword on little feet, with three-fold
separate flame above the hilt, inhabiting

   fire eating into air. Thus nested
in the phosphorescent alligator that copies each
   digression of the shape, he pants and settles—head
up and eyes black as the molested bird's, with look of whetted
                                                  fierceness,

in what is merely
   breathing and recoiling from the hand.
Thinking himself hid among the yet unfound jade ax-heads,
   silver jaguars and bats, and amethysts and
polished iron, gold in a ten-ton chain, and pearls the size of pigeon-
                                                  eggs,

he is alive there
   in his basilisk cocoon beneath
the one of living green; his quicksilver ferocity
   quenched in the rustle of his fall into the sheath
which is the shattering sudden splash that marks his temporary
                                                  loss.

THE FRIGATE PELICAN

Rapidly cruising or lying on the air there is a bird
    that realizes Rasselas's friend's project
    of wings uniting levity with strength. This
        hell-diver, frigate-bird, hurricane-
bird; unless swift is the proper word
        for him, the storm omen when
        he flies close to the waves, should be seen
           fishing, although oftener
           he appears to prefer

to take, on the wing, from industrious crude-winged species,
    the fish they have caught, and is seldom successless.
    A marvel of grace, no matter how fast his
        victim may fly or how often may
turn. The others with similar ease,
    slowly rising once more,
        move out to the top
        of the circle and stop

and blow back, allowing the wind to reverse their direction—
    unlike the more stalwart swan that can ferry the
    woodcutter's two children home. Make hay; keep
        the shop; I have one sheep; were a less
limber animal's mottoes. This one
        finds sticks for the swan's-down-dress
    of his child to rest upon and would
        not know Gretel from Hänsel.
        As impassioned Handel—

meant for a lawyer and a masculine German domestic
    career—clandestinely studied the harpsichord
    and never was known to have fallen in love,
        the unconfiding frigate-bird hides

in the height and in the majestic
    display of his art. He glides
  a hundred feet or quivers about
      as charred paper behaves—full
      of feints; and an eagle

of vigilance. . . . *Festina lente.* Be gay
    civilly? How so? "If I do well I am blessed
    whether any bless me or not, and if I do
        ill I am cursed." We watch the moon rise
on the Susquehanna. In his way,
    this most romantic bird flies
to a more mundane place, the mangrove
    swamp to sleep. He wastes the moon.
    But he, and others, soon

rise from the bough and though flying, are able to foil the tired
    moment of danger that lays on heart and lungs the
    weight of the python that crushes to powder.

THE BUFFALO

　　　Black in blazonry means
prudence; and niger, unpropitious. Might
hematite—
　　　black, compactly incurved horns on bison
　　　　　have significance? The
　　　soot-brown tail-tuft on
　　　　　　a kind of lion-

　　　　tail; what would that express?
And John Steuart Curry's Ajax pulling
grass—no ring
　　　in his nose—two birds standing on the back?

　　　　　　.　　　　.　　　.

　　　The modern
ox does not look like the Augsburg ox's
portrait. Yes,
　　　the great extinct wild Aurochs was a beast
　　　　　to paint, with stripe and six-
　　　foot horn-spread—decreased
　　　　　　tó Siamese-cat-

　　　Brown Swiss size or zebu-
shape, with white plush dewlap and warm-blooded
hump; to red-
　　　skinned Hereford or to piebald Holstein. Yet
　　　　　some would say the sparse-haired
　　　buffalo has met
　　　　　　human notions best—

　　　　unlike the elephant,
both jewel and jeweller in the hairs
that he wears—

(27

no white-nosed Vermont ox yoked with its twin
    to haul the maple-sap,
up to their knees in
        snow; no freakishly

Over-Drove Ox drawn by
Rowlandson, but the Indian buffalo,
albino-
    footed, standing in a mud-lake with a
        day's work to do. No white
Christian heathen, way-
        laid by the Buddha,

    serves him so well as the
buffalo—as mettlesome as if check-
reined—free neck
    stretching out, and snake tail in a half-twist
        on the flank; nor will so
cheerfully assist
        the Sage sitting with

    feet at the same side, to
dismount at the shrine; nor are there any
ivory
    tusks like those two horns which when a tiger
        coughs, are lowered fiercely
and convert the fur
        to harmless rubbish.

    The Indian buffalo,
led by bare-leggèd herd-boys to a hay
hut where they
    stable it, need not fear comparison
        with bison, with the twins,
    indeed with any
        of ox ancestry.

NINE NECTARINES

Arranged by two's as peaches are,
at intervals that all may live—
eight and a single one, on twigs that
grew the year before—they look like
a derivative;
although not uncommonly
the opposite is seen—
nine peaches on a nectarine.
Fuzzless through slender crescent leaves
of green or blue or
both, in the Chinese style, the four

pairs' half-moon leaf-mosaic turns
out to the sun the sprinkled blush
of puce-American-Beauty pink
applied to bees-wax gray by the
uninquiring brush
of mercantile bookbinding.
Like the peach *Yu*, the red-
cheeked peach which cannot aid the dead,
but eaten in time prevents death,
the Italian
peach-nut, Persian plum, Ispahan

secluded wall-grown nectarine,
as wild spontaneous fruit was
found in China first. But was it wild?
Prudent de Candolle would not say.
One perceives no flaws
in this emblematic group
of nine, with leaf window
unquilted by *curculio*
which someone once depicted on

this much-mended plate
or in the also accurate

unantlered moose or Iceland horse
or ass asleep against the old
thick, low-leaning nectarine that is the
color of the shrub-tree's brownish
flower.

  . .. .

A Chinese "understands
the spirit of the wilderness"
and the nectarine-loving kylin
of pony appearance—the long-
tailed or the tailless
small cinnamon-brown, common
camel-haired unicorn
with antelope feet and no horn,
here enameled on porcelain.
It was a Chinese
who imagined this masterpiece.

TO A PRIZE BIRD

You suit me well, for you can make me laugh,
nor are you blinded by the chaff
   that every wind sends spinning from the rick.

You know to think, and what you think you speak
with much of Samson's pride and bleak
   finality, and none dare bid you stop.

Pride sits you well, so strut, colossal bird.
No barnyard makes you look absurd;
   your brazen claws are staunch against defeat.

THE FISH

wade
through black jade.
   Of the crow-blue mussel-shells, one keeps
   adjusting the ash-heaps;
      opening and shutting itself like

an
injured fan.
   The barnacles which encrust the side
   of the wave, cannot hide
      there for the submerged shafts of the

sun,
split like spun
   glass, move themselves with spotlight swiftness
   into the crevices—
      in and out, illuminating

the
turquoise sea
   of bodies. The water drives a wedge
   of iron through the iron edge
      of the cliff; whereupon the stars,

pink
rice-grains, ink-
   bespattered jelly-fish, crabs like green
   lilies, and submarine
      toadstools, slide each on the other.

All
external
   marks of abuse are present on this

defiant edifice—
   all the physical features of

ac-
cident—lack
   of cornice, dynamite grooves, burns, and
   hatchet strokes, these things stand
      out on it; the chasm-side is

dead.
Repeated
   evidence has proved that it can live
   on what can not revive
      its youth. The sea grows old in it.

IN THIS AGE OF HARD TRYING,
NONCHALANCE IS GOOD AND

"really, it is not the
    business of the gods to bake clay pots." They did not
        do it in this instance. A few
           revolved upon the axes of their worth
    as if excessive popularity might be a pot;

they did not venture the
    profession of humility. The polished wedge
        that might have split the firmament
           was dumb. At last it threw itself away
    and falling down, conferred on some poor fool, a privilege.

"Taller by the length of
    a conversation of five hundred years than all
        the others," there was one, whose tales
           of what could never have been actual—
    were better than the haggish, uncompanionable drawl

of certitude; his by-
    play was more terrible in its effectiveness
        than the fiercest frontal attack.
           The staff, the bag, the feigned inconsequence
    of manner, best bespeak that weapon, self-protectiveness.

TO STATECRAFT EMBALMED

There is nothing to be said for you. Guard
your secret. Conceal it under your hard
    plumage, necromancer.
       O
bird, whose tents were "awnings of Egyptian
yarn," shall Justice' faint zigzag inscription—
    leaning like a dancer—
       show
the pulse of its once vivid sovereignty?
You say not, and transmigrating from the
    sarcophagus, you wind
       snow
silence round us and with moribund talk,
half limping and half-ladyfied, you stalk
    about. Ibis, we find
       no
virtue in you—alive and yet so dumb.
Discreet behavior is not now the sum
    of statesmanlike good sense.
       Though
it were the incarnation of dead grace?
As if a death mask ever could replace
    life's faulty excellence!
       Slow
to remark the steep, too strict proportion
of your throne, you'll see the wrenched distortion
    of suicidal dreams
       go
staggering toward itself and with its bill
attack its own identity, until
    foe seems friend and friend seems
       foe.

POETRY

I, too, dislike it.
　　Reading it, however, with a perfect contempt for it, one dis-
　　　　　　　　　　　　　　　　　　　　　　　covers in
　　it, after all, a place for the genuine.

PEDANTIC LITERALIST

Prince Rupert's drop, paper muslin ghost,
  white torch—"with power to say unkind
things with kindness, and the most
    irritating things in the midst of love and
     tears," you invite destruction.

You are like the meditative man
  with the perfunctory heart; its
carved cordiality ran
    to and fro at first like an inlaid and royal
     immutable production;

then afterward "neglected to be
  painful, deluding him with
loitering formality,"
    "doing its duty as if it did it not,"
     presenting an obstruction

to the motive that it served. What stood
  erect in you has withered. A
little "palm-tree of turned wood"
    informs your once spontaneous core in its
     immutable production.

CRITICS AND CONNOISSEURS

There is a great amount of poetry in unconscious
fastidiousness. Certain Ming
products, imperial floor-coverings of coach-
wheel yellow, are well enough in their way but I have seen
something
that I like better—a
mere childish attempt to make an imperfectly bal-
lasted animal stand up,
similar determination to make a pup
eat his meat from the plate.

I remember a swan under the willows in Oxford,
with flamingo-colored, maple-
leaflike feet. It reconnoitered like a battle-
ship. Disbelief and conscious fastidiousness were
ingredients in its
disinclination to move. Finally its hardihood was
not proof against its
proclivity to more fully appraise such bits
of food as the stream

bore counter to it; it made away with what I gave it
to eat. I have seen this swan and
I have seen you; I have seen ambition without
understanding in a variety of forms. Happening to stand
by an ant-hill, I have
seen a fastidious ant carrying a stick north, south,
east, west, till it turned on
itself, struck out from the flower-bed into the lawn,
and returned to the point

from which it had started. Then abandoning the stick as
useless and overtaxing its

jaws with a particle of whitewash—pill-like but
heavy, it again went through the same course of procedure.
What is
there in being able
to say that one has dominated the stream in an attitude
of self-defense;
in proving that one has had the experience
of carrying a stick?

THE MONKEYS

winked too much and were afraid of snakes. The zebras,
                                        supreme in
their abnormality; the elephants with their fog-colored skin
    and strictly practical appendages
        were there, the small cats; and the parakeet—
            trivial and humdrum on examination, destroying
        bark and portions of the food it could not eat.

I recall their magnificence, now not more magnificent
than it is dim. It is difficult to recall the ornament,
    speech, and precise manner of what one might
        call the minor acquaintances twenty
            years back; but I shall not forget him—that Gilgamesh
                                        among
        the hairy carnivora—that cat with the

wedge-shaped, slate-gray marks on its forelegs and the resolute
                                        tail,
astringently remarking, "They have imposed on us with their pale
    half-fledged protestations, trembling about
        in inarticulate frenzy, saying
            it is not for us to understand art; finding it
        all so difficult, examining the thing

as if it were inconceivably arcanic, as symmet-
rically frigid as if it had been carved out of chrysoprase
    or marble—strict with tension, malignant
        in its power over us and deeper
            than the sea when it proffers flattery in exchange for
                                        hemp,
        rye, flax, horses, platinum, timber, and fur."

40)

IN THE DAYS OF PRISMATIC COLOR

not in the days of Adam and Eve, but when Adam
   was alone; when there was no smoke and color was
fine, not with the refinement
   of early civilization art, but because
of its originality; with nothing to modify it but the

mist that went up, obliqueness was a variation
   of the perpendicular, plain to see and
to account for: it is no
   longer that; nor did the blue-red-yellow band
of incandescence that was color keep its stripe: it also is one of

those things into which much that is peculiar can be
   read; complexity is not a crime, but carry
it to the point of murkiness
   and nothing is plain. Complexity,
moreover, that has been committed to darkness, instead of

granting itself to be the pestilence that it is, moves all a-
   bout as if to bewilder us with the dismal
fallacy that insistence
   is the measure of achievement and that all
truth must be dark. Principally throat, sophistication is as it al-

ways has been—at the antipodes from the init-
   ial great truths. "Part of it was crawling, part of it
was about to crawl, the rest
   was torpid in its lair." In the short-legged, fit-
ful advance, the gurgling and all the minutiae—we have the
                                   classic

multitude of feet. To what purpose! Truth is no Apollo
Belvedere, no formal thing. The wave may go over it if it likes.
Know that it will be there when it says,
"I shall be there when the wave has gone by."

PETER

       Strong and slippery,
built for the midnight grass-party
confronted by four cats, he sleeps his time away—
the detached first claw on the foreleg corresponding
to the thumb, retracted to its tip; the small tuft of fronds
or katydid-legs above each eye numbering all units
in each group; the shadbones regularly set about the mouth
to droop or rise in unison like porcupine-quills.
He lets himself be flattened out by gravity,
as seaweed is tamed and weakened by the sun,
compelled when extended, to lie stationary.
Sleep is the result of his delusion that one must
do as well as one can for oneself,
sleep—epitome of what is to him the end of life.
Demonstrate on him how the lady placed a forked stick
on the innocuous neck-sides of the dangerous southern snake.
One need not try to stir him up; his prune-shaped head
and alligator-eyes are not party to the joke.
Lifted and handled, he may be dangled like an eel
or set up on the forearm like a mouse;
his eyes bisected by pupils of a pin's width,
are flickeringly exhibited, then covered up.
May be? I should have said might have been;
when he has been got the better of in a dream—
as in a fight with nature or with cats, we all know it.
Profound sleep is not with him a fixed illusion.
Springing about with froglike accuracy, with jerky cries
when taken in hand, he is himself again;
to sit caged by the rungs of a domestic chair
would be unprofitable—human. What is the good of hypocrisy?
It is permissible to choose one's employment,
to abandon the nail, or roly-poly,
when it shows signs of being no longer a pleasure,

to score the nearby magazine with a double line of strokes.
He can talk but insolently says nothing. What of it?
When one is frank, one's very presence is a compliment.
It is clear that he can see the virtue of naturalness,
that he does not regard the published fact as a surrender.
As for the disposition invariably to affront,
an animal with claws should have an opportunity to use them.
The eel-like extension of trunk into tail is not an accident.
To leap, to lengthen out, divide the air, to purloin, to pursue.
To tell the hen: fly over the fence, go in the wrong way
in your perturbation—this is life;
to do less would be nothing but dishonesty.

PICKING AND CHOOSING

Literature is a phase of life. If one is afraid of it,
the situation is irremediable; if one approaches it familiarly,
what one says of it is worthless.
The opaque allusion, the simulated flight upward,
accomplishes nothing. Why cloud the fact
that Shaw is self-conscious in the field of sentiment
but is otherwise rewarding; that James
is all that has been said of him. It is not Hardy the novelist
and Hardy the poet, but one man interpreting life as emotion.
The critic should know what he likes:
Gordon Craig with his "this is I" and "this is mine,"
with his three wise men, his "sad French greens," and his
"Chinese cherry"
Gordon Craig so inclinational and unashamed—a critic.
And Burke is a psychologist, of acute racoon-like curiosity.
Summa Diligentia; to the humbug whose name is so amusing—
very young and very rushed, Caesar crossed the Alps
on the top of a "*diligence*"!
We are not daft about the meaning,
but this familiarity with wrong meanings puzzles one.
Humming-bug, the candles are not wired for electricity.
Small dog, going over the lawn nipping the linen and saying
that you have a badger—remember Xenophon;
only rudimentary behavior is necessary to put us on the scent.
"A right good salvo of barks," a few strong wrinkles puckering
the skin between the ears, is all we ask.

ENGLAND

with its baby rivers and little towns, each with its abbey or its
cathedral,
with voices—one voice perhaps, echoing through the transept—
the
criterion of suitability and convenience: and Italy
with its equal shores—contriving an epicureanism
from which the grossness has been extracted:

and Greece with its goat and its gourds,
the nest of modified illusions: and France,
the "chrysalis of the nocturnal butterfly,"
in whose products mystery of construction
diverts one from what was originally one's object—
substance at the core: and the East with its snails, its emotional

shorthand and jade cockroaches, its rock crystal and its
imperturbability,
all of museum quality: and America where there
is the little old ramshackle victoria in the south,
where cigars are smoked on the street in the north;
where there are no proof-readers, no silkworms, no digressions;

the wild man's land; grassless, linksless, languageless country in
which letters are written
not in Spanish, not in Greek, not in Latin, not in shorthand,
but in plain American which cats and dogs can read!
The letter *a* in psalm and calm when
pronounced with the sound of *a* in candle, is very noticeable, but

why should continents of misapprehension
have to be accounted for by the fact?
Does it follow that because there are poisonous toadstools

which resemble mushrooms, both are dangerous?
Of mettlesomeness which may be mistaken for appetite,
of heat which may appear to be haste,
no conclusions may be drawn.

To have misapprehended the matter is to have confessed that
                              one has not looked far enough.
The sublimated wisdom of China, Egyptian discernment,
the cataclysmic torrent of emotion
compressed in the verbs of the Hebrew language,
the books of the man who is able to say,
"I envy nobody but him, and him only,
who catches more fish than I do"—
the flower and fruit of all that noted superiority—
if not stumbled upon in America,
must one imagine that it is not there?
It has never been confined to one locality.

WHEN I BUY PICTURES

or what is closer to the truth,
when I look at that of which I may regard myself as the
                                        imaginary possessor,
I fix upon what would give me pleasure in my average moments:
the satire upon curiosity in which no more is discernible
than the intensity of the mood;
or quite the opposite—the old thing, the medieval decorated
                                        hat-box
in which there are hounds with waists diminishing like the
                                        waist of the hour-glass,
and deer and birds and seated people;
it may be no more than a square of parquetry; the literal
                                        biography perhaps,
in letters standing well apart upon a parchment-like expanse;
an artichoke in six varieties of blue; the snipe-legged
                                        hieroglyphic in three parts;
the silver fence protecting Adam's grave, or Michael taking
                                        Adam by the wrist.
Too stern an intellectual emphasis upon this quality or that
                                        detracts from one's enjoyment.
It must not wish to disarm anything; nor may the approved
                                        triumph easily be honored—
that which is great because something else is small.
It comes to this: of whatever sort it is,
it must be "lit with piercing glances into the life of things";
it must acknowledge the spiritual forces which have made it.

A GRAVE

Man looking into the sea,
taking the view from those who have as much right to it as
                                              you have to it yourself,
it is human nature to stand in the middle of a thing,
but you cannot stand in the middle of this;
the sea has nothing to give but a well excavated grave.
The firs stand in a procession, each with an emerald turkey-
                                              foot at the top,
reserved as their contours, saying nothing;
repression, however, is not the most obvious characteristic of
                                              the sea;
the sea is a collector, quick to return a rapacious look.
There are others besides you who have worn that look—
whose expression is no longer a protest; the fish no longer
                                              investigate them
for their bones have not lasted:
men lower nets, unconscious of the fact that they are
                                              desecrating a grave,
and row quickly away—the blades of the oars
moving together like the feet of water-spiders as if there were
                                              no such thing as death.
The wrinkles progress among themselves in a phalanx—
                                              beautiful under networks of foam,
and fade breathlessly while the sea rustles in and out of the
                                              seaweed;
the birds swim through the air at top speed, emitting cat-calls
                                              as heretofore—
the tortoise-shell scourges about the feet of the cliffs, in motion
                                              beneath them;
and the ocean, under the pulsation of lighthouses and noise of
                                              bell-buoys,

advances as usual, looking as if it were not that ocean in which
              dropped things are bound to sink—
in which if they turn and twist, it is neither with volition nor
              consciousness.

THOSE VARIOUS SCALPELS,

those
various sounds consistently indistinct, like intermingled echoes
   struck from thin glasses successively at random—
      the inflection disguised: your hair, the tails of two
   fighting-cocks head to head in stone —
      like sculptured scimitars repeating the curve of your ears in
                           reverse order:
     your eyes, flowers of ice and snow

sown by tearing winds on the cordage of disabled ships; your
                             raised hand,
   an ambiguous signature: your cheeks, those rosettes
   of blood on the stone floors of French châteaux,
  with regard to which the guides are so affirmative—
     your other hand,

a bundle of lances all alike, partly hid by emeralds from Persia
   and the fractional magnificence of Florentine
     goldwork—a collection of little objects—
  sapphires set with emeralds, and pearls with a moonstone,
                            made fine
   with enamel in gray, yellow, and dragon-fly blue;
     a lemon, a pear

and three bunches of grapes, tied with silver: your dress, a
                          magnificent square
  cathedral tower of uniform
   and at the same time diverse appearance—a
 species of vertical vineyard rustling in the storm
   of conventional opinion. Are they weapons or scalpels?
    Whetted to brilliance

by the hard majesty of that sophistication which is superior to
                                                              opportunity,
these things are rich instruments with which to experiment.
But why dissect destiny with instruments
    more highly specialized than components of destiny itself?

THE LABORS OF HERCULES

To popularize the mule, its neat exterior
expressing the principle of accommodation reduced to a
                                        minimum:
to persuade one of austere taste, proud in the possession of home,
                                and a musician—
that the piano is a free field for etching; that his "charming
                                    tadpole notes"
belong to the past when one had time to play them:
to persuade those self-wrought Midases of brains
whose fourteen-carat ignorance aspires to rise in value,
                                augurs disappointment,
that one must not borrow a long white beard and tie it on
and threaten with the scythe of time the casually curious:
to teach the bard with too elastic a selectiveness
that one detects creative power by its capacity to conquer one's
                                        detachment,
that while it may have more elasticity than logic;
it flies along in a straight line like electricity,
depopulating areas that boast of their remoteness,
to prove to the high priests of caste
that snobbishness is a stupidity,
the best side out, of age-old toadyism,
kissing the feet of the man above,
kicking the face of the man below;
to teach the patron-saints-to-atheists
that we are sick of the earth,
sick of the pig-sty, wild geese and wild men;
to convince snake-charming controversialists
that one keeps on knowing
"that the Negro is not brutal,
that the Jew is not greedy,
that the Oriental is not immoral,
that the German is not a Hun."

NEW YORK

the savage's romance,
accreted where we need the space for commerce—
the center of the wholesale fur trade,
starred with tepees of ermine and peopled with foxes,
the long guard-hairs waving two inches beyond the body of the
                                                                pelt;
the ground dotted with deer-skins—white with white spots,
"as satin needlework in a single color may carry a varied
                                                        pattern,"
and wilting eagle's-down compacted by the wind;
and picardels of beaver-skin; white ones alert with snow.
It is a far cry from the "queen full of jewels"
and the beau with the muff,
from the gilt coach shaped like a perfume-bottle,
to the conjunction of the Monongahela and the Allegheny,
and the scholastic philosophy of the wilderness.
It is not the dime-novel exterior,
Niagara Falls, the calico horses and the war-canoe;
it is not that "if the fur is not finer than such as one sees others
                                                                wear,
one would rather be without it"—
that estimated in raw meat and berries, we could feed the
                                                            universe;
it is not the atmosphere of ingenuity,
the otter, the beaver, the puma skins
without shooting-irons or dogs;
it is not the plunder,
but "accessibility to experience."

PEOPLE'S SURROUNDINGS

They answer one's questions,
a deal table compact with the wall;
in this dried bone of arrangement
one's "natural promptness" is compressed, not crowded out;
one's style is not lost in such simplicity.

The palace furniture, so old-fashioned, so old-fashionable;
Sèvres china and the fireplace dogs—
bronze dromios with pointed ears, as obsolete as pugs;
one has one's preferences in the matter of bad furniture,
and this is not one's choice.

The vast indestructible necropolis
of composite Yawman-Erbe separable units;
the steel, the oak, the glass, the Poor Richard publications
containing the public secrets of efficiency
on paper so thin that "one thousand four hundred and twenty
                                  pages make one inch,"
exclaiming, so to speak, When you take my time, you take
                                  something I had meant to use;

the highway hid by fir-trees in rhododendron twenty feet deep,
the peacocks, hand-forged gates, old Persian velvet,
roses outlined in pale black on an ivory ground,
the pierced iron shadows of the cedars,
Chinese carved glass, old Waterford, lettered ladies;
landscape gardening twisted into permanence;

straight lines over such great distances as one finds in Utah or
                                  in Texas,
where people do not have to be told
that a good brake is as important as a good motor;
where by means of extra sense-cells in the skin

they can, like trout, smell what is coming—
those cool sirs with the explicit sensory apparatus of common
                                                        sense,
who know the exact distance between two points as the crow
                                                        flies;
there is something attractive about a mind that moves in a
                                                straight line—
the municipal bat-roost of mosquito warfare;
the American string quartet;
these are questions more than answers,

and Bluebeard's Tower above the coral-reefs,
the magic mouse-trap closing on all points of the compass,
capping like petrified surf the furious azure of the bay,
where there is no dust, and life is like a lemon-leaf,
a green piece of tough translucent parchment,
where the crimson, the copper, and the Chinese vermilion of
                                                the poincianas
set fire to the masonry and turquoise blues refute the clock;
this dungeon with odd notions of hospitality,
with its "chessmen carved out of moonstones,"
its mocking-birds, fringed lilies, and hibiscus,
its black butterflies with blue half circles on their wings,
tan goats with onyx ears, its lizards glittering and without
                                                thickness,
like splashes of fire and silver on the pierced turquoise of the
                                                lattices
and the acacia-like lady shivering at the touch of a hand,
lost in a small collision of the orchids—
dyed quicksilver let fall,
to disappear like an obedient chameleon in fifty shades of mauve
                                                and amethyst.
Here where the mind of this establishment has come to the
                                                conclusion

that it would be impossible to revolve about oneself too much,
sophistication has, "like an escalator," "cut the nerve of progress."

In these non-committal, personal-impersonal expressions of
                                                        appearance,
the eye knows what to skip;
the physiognomy of conduct must not reveal the skeleton;
"a setting must not have the air of being one,"
yet with X-ray-like inquisitive intensity upon it, the surfaces
                                                        go back;
the interfering fringes of expression are but a stain on what
                                                        stands out,
there is neither up nor down to it;
we see the exterior and the fundamental structure—
captains of armies, cooks, carpenters,
cutlers, gamesters, surgeons and armorers,
lapidaries, silkmen, glovers, fiddlers and ballad-singers,
sextons of churches, dyers of black cloth, hostlers and chimney-
                                                        sweeps,
queens, countesses, ladies, emperors, travelers and mariners,
dukes, princes and gentlemen,
in their respective places—
camps, forges and battlefields,
conventions, oratories and wardrobes,
dens, deserts, railway stations, asylums and places where
                                                        engines are made,
shops, prisons, brickyards and altars of churches—
in magnificent places clean and decent,
castles, palaces, dining-halls, theaters and imperial audience-
                                                        chambers.

SNAKES, MONGOOSES, SNAKE-CHARMERS, AND THE LIKE

I have a friend who would give a price for those long fingers all
                                                    of one length—
those hideous bird's claws, for that exotic asp and the mongoose—
products of the country in which everything is hard work, the
                                        country of the grass-getter,
the torch-bearer, the dog-servant, the messenger-bearer, the
                                                        holy-man.
Engrossed in this distinguished worm nearly as wild and as
                                fierce as the day it was caught,
he gazes as if incapable of looking at anything with a view to
                                                        analysis.
"The slight snake rippling quickly through the grass,
the leisurely tortoise with its pied back,
the chameleon passing from twig to stone, from stone to straw,"
lit his imagination at one time; his admiration now converges
                                                        upon this.
Thick, not heavy, it stands up from its traveling-basket,
the essentially Greek, the plastic animal all of a piece from nose
                                                        to tail;
one is compelled to look at it as at the shadows of the alps
imprisoning in their folds like flies in amber, the rhythms of
                                                the skating-rink.
This animal to which from the earliest times, importance has
                                                        attached,
fine as its worshipers have said—for what was it invented?
To show that when intelligence in its pure form
has embarked on a train of thought which is unproductive, it
                                                will come back?
We do not know; the only positive thing about it is its shape;
                                                but why protest?
The passion for setting people right is in itself an afflictive disease.
Distaste which takes no credit to itself is best.

BOWLS

on the green
with lignum vitae balls and ivory markers,
the pins planted in wild duck formation,
and quickly dispersed—
by this survival of ancient punctilio
in the manner of Chinese lacquer-carving,
layer after layer exposed by certainty of touch and unhurried
                                                              incision
so that only so much color shall be revealed as is necessary to
                                                        the picture,
I learn that we are precisionists,
not citizens of Pompeii arrested in action
as a cross-section of one's correspondence would seem to imply.
Renouncing a policy of boorish indifference
to everything that has been said since the days of Matilda,
I shall purchase an etymological dictionary of modern English
that I may understand what is written,
and like the ant and the spider
returning from time to time to headquarters,
shall answer the question
"why do I like winter better than I like summer?"
and acknowledge that it does not make me sick
to look playwrights and poets and novelists straight in the face—
that I feel just the same;
and I shall write to the publisher of the magazine
which will "appear the first day of the month
and disappear before one has had time to buy it
unless one takes proper precaution,"
and make an effort to please—
since he who gives quickly gives twice
in nothing so much as in a letter.

NOVICES

anatomize their work
in the sense in which Will Honeycomb was jilted by a duchess;
the little assumptions of the scared ego confusing the issue
so that they do not know "whether it is the buyer or the seller
                                    who gives the money"—
an abstruse idea plain to none but the artist,
the only seller who buys, and holds on to the money.
Because one expresses oneself and entitles it wisdom, one is not
                                    a fool. What an idea!
"Dracontine cockatrices, perfect and poisonous from the
                                    beginning,"
they present themselves as a contrast to sea-serpented regions
                "unlit by the half-lights of more conscious art."

Acquiring at thirty what at sixty they will be trying to forget,
blind to the right word, deaf to satire
which like "the smell of the cypress strengthens the nerves of
                                    the brain,"
averse from the antique
with "that tinge of sadness about it which a reflective mind
                                    always feels,
it is so little and so much"—
they write the sort of thing that would in their judgment
                                    interest a lady;
curious to know if we do not adore each letter of the alphabet
                that goes to make a word of it—
according to the Act of Congress, the sworn statement of the
                treasurer and all the rest of it—
the counterpart to what we are:
stupid man; men are strong and no one pays any attention:
stupid woman; women have charm, and how annoying they
                                    can be.
Yes, "the authors are wonderful people, particularly those that
                                    write the most,"

the masters of all languages, the supertadpoles of expression.
Accustomed to the recurring phosphorescence of antiquity,
the "much noble vagueness and indefinite jargon" of Plato,
the lucid movements of the royal yacht upon the learned
                                        scenery of Egypt—
king, steward, and harper, seated amidships while the jade and
                        the rock crystal course about in solution,

their suavity surmounts the surf—
the willowy wit, the transparent equation of Isaiah, Jeremiah,
                                        Ezekiel, Daniel.
Bored by "the detailless perspective of the sea," reiterative and
                                                naïve,
and its chaos of rocks—the stuffy remarks of the Hebrews—
the good and alive young men demonstrate the assertion
that it is not necessary to be associated with that which has
                                        annoyed one;
they have never made a statement which they found so easy
                                        to prove—
"split like a glass against a wall"
in this "precipitate of dazzling impressions,
the spontaneous unforced passion of the Hebrew language—
an abyss of verbs full of reverberations and tempestuous energy"
in which action perpetuates action and angle is at variance with
                                        angle
till submerged by the general action;
obscured by "fathomless suggestions of color,"
by incessantly panting lines of green, white with concussion,
in this drama of water against rocks—this "ocean of hurrying
                                        consonants"
with its "great livid stains like long slabs of green marble,"
its "flashing lances of perpendicular lightning" and "molten
                                        fires swallowed up,"
"with foam on its barriers,"
"crashing itself out in one long hiss of spray."

MARRIAGE

This institution,
perhaps one should say enterprise
out of respect for which
one says one need not change one's mind
about a thing one has believed in,
requiring public promises
of one's intention
to fulfil a private obligation:
I wonder what Adam and Eve
think of it by this time,
this fire-gilt steel
alive with goldenness;
how bright it shows—
"of circular traditions and impostures,
committing many spoils,"
requiring all one's criminal ingenuity
to avoid!
Psychology which explains everything
explains nothing,
and we are still in doubt.
Eve: beautiful woman—
I have seen her
when she was so handsome
she gave me a start,
able to write simultaneously
in three languages—
English, German and French—
and talk in the meantime;
equally positive in demanding a commotion
and in stipulating quiet:
"*I* should like to be alone";
to which the visitor replies,
"I should like to be alone;

why not be alone together?"
Below the incandescent stars
below the incandescent fruit,
the strange experience of beauty;
its existence is too much;
it tears one to pieces
and each fresh wave of consciousness
is poison.
"See her, see her in this common world,"
the central flaw
in that first crystal-fine experiment,
this amalgamation which can never be more
than an interesting impossibility,
describing it
as "that strange paradise
unlike flesh, stones,
gold or stately buildings,
the choicest piece of my life:
the heart rising
in its estate of peace
as a boat rises
with the rising of the water";
constrained in speaking of the serpent—
shed snakeskin in the history of politeness
not to be returned to again—
that invaluable accident
exonerating Adam.
And he has beauty also;
it's distressing—the O thou
to whom from whom,
without whom nothing—Adam;
"something feline,
something colubrine"—how true!
a crouching mythological monster
in that Persian miniature of emerald mines,
raw silk—ivory white, snow white,
oyster white and six others—

that paddock full of leopards and giraffes—
long lemon-yellow bodies
sown with trapezoids of blue.
Alive with words,
vibrating like a cymbal
touched before it has been struck,
he has prophesied correctly—
the industrious waterfall,
"the speedy stream
which violently bears all before it,
at one time silent as the air
and now as powerful as the wind."
"Treading chasms
on the uncertain footing of a spear,"
forgetting that there is in woman
a quality of mind
which as an instinctive manifestation
is unsafe,
he goes on speaking
in a formal customary strain,
of "past states, the present state,
seals, promises,
the evil one suffered,
the good one enjoys,
hell, heaven,
everything convenient
to promote one's joy."
In him a state of mind
perceives what it was not
intended that he should;
"he experiences a solemn joy
in seeing that he has become an idol."
Plagued by the nightingale
in the new leaves,
with its silence—
not its silence but its silences,

he says of it:
"It clothes me with a shirt of fire."
"He dares not clap his hands
to make it go on
lest it should fly off;
if he does nothing, it will sleep;
if he cries out, it will not understand."
Unnerved by the nightingale
and dazzled by the apple,
impelled by "the illusion of a fire
effectual to extinguish fire,"
compared with which
the shining of the earth
is but deformity—a fire
"as high as deep
as bright as broad
as long as life itself,"
he stumbles over marriage,
"a very trivial object indeed"
to have destroyed the attitude
in which he stood—
the ease of the philosopher
unfathered by a woman.
Unhelpful Hymen!
a kind of overgrown cupid
reduced to insignificance
by the mechanical advertising
parading as involuntary comment,
by that experiment of Adam's
with ways out but no way in—
the ritual of marriage,
augmenting all its lavishness;
its fiddle-head ferns,
lotus flowers, opuntias, white dromedaries,
its hippopotamus—
nose and mouth combined

in one magnificent hopper—
its snake and the potent apple.
He tells us
that "for love that will
gaze an eagle blind,
that is with Hercules
climbing the trees
in the garden of the Hesperides,
from forty-five to seventy
is the best age,"
commending it
as a fine art, as an experiment,
a duty or as merely recreation.
One must not call him ruffian
nor friction a calamity—
the fight to be affectionate:
"no truth can be fully known
until it has been tried
by the tooth of disputation."
The blue panther with black eyes,
the basalt panther with blue eyes,
entirely graceful—
one must give them the path—
the black obsidian Diana
who "darkeneth her countenance
as a bear doth,"
the spiked hand
that has an affection for one
and proves it to the bone,
impatient to assure you
that impatience is the mark of independence,
not of bondage.
"Married people often look that way"—
"seldom and cold, up and down,
mixed and malarial
with a good day and a bad."

We Occidentals are so unemotional,
self lost, the irony preserved
in "the Ahasuerus *tête-à-tête* banquet"
with its small orchids like snakes' tongues,
with its "good monster, lead the way,"
with little laughter
and munificence of humor
in that quixotic atmosphere of frankness
in which "four o'clock does not exist,
but at five o'clock
the ladies in their imperious humility
are ready to receive you";
in which experience attests
that men have power
and sometimes one is made to feel it.
He says, "What monarch would not blush
to have a wife
with hair like a shaving-brush?"
The fact of woman
is "not the sound of the flute
but very poison."
She says, "Men are monopolists
of 'stars, garters, buttons
and other shining baubles'—
unfit to be the guardians
of another person's happiness."
He says, "These mummies
must be handled carefully—
'the crumbs from a lion's meal,
a couple of shins and the bit of an ear';
turn to the letter M
and you will find
that 'a wife is a coffin,'
that severe object
with the pleasing geometry
stipulating space not people,

refusing to be buried
and uniquely disappointing,
revengefully wrought in the attitude
of an adoring child
to a distinguished parent."
She says, "This butterfly,
this waterfly, this nomad
that has 'proposed
to settle on my hand for life'—
What can one do with it?
There must have been more time
in Shakespeare's day
to sit and watch a play.
You know so many artists who are fools."
He says, "You know so many fools
who are not artists."
The fact forgot
that "some have merely rights
while some have obligations,"
he loves himself so much,
he can permit himself
no rival in that love.
She loves herself so much,
she cannot see herself enough—
a statuette of ivory on ivory,
the logical last touch
to an expansive splendor
earned as wages for work done:
one is not rich but poor
when one can always seem so right.
What can one do for them—
these savages
condemned to disaffect
all those who are not visionaries
alert to undertake the silly task
of making people noble?

This model of petrine fidelity
who "leaves her peaceful husband
only because she has seen enough of him"—
that orator reminding you,
"I am yours to command."
"Everything to do with love is mystery;
it is more than a day's work
to investigate this science."
One sees that it is rare—
that striking grasp of opposites
opposed each to the other, not to unity,
which in cycloid inclusiveness
has dwarfed the demonstration
of Columbus with the egg—
a triumph of simplicity—
that charitive Euroclydon
of frightening disinterestedness
which the world hates,
admitting:

   "I am such a cow,
   if I had a sorrow
   I should feel it a long time;
   I am not one of those
   who have a great sorrow
   in the morning
   and a great joy at noon";

which says: "I have encountered it
among those unpretentious
protégés of wisdom,
where seeming to parade
as the debater and the Roman,
the statesmanship
of an archaic Daniel Webster
persists to their simplicity of temper

as the essence of the matter:

   'Liberty and union
   now and forever';

the Book on the writing-table;
the hand in the breast-pocket."

AN OCTOPUS

of ice. Deceptively reserved and flat,
it lies "in grandeur and in mass"
beneath a sea of shifting snow-dunes;
dots of cyclamen-red and maroon on its clearly defined

pseudo-podia
made of glass that will bend—a much needed invention—
comprising twenty-eight ice-fields from fifty to five hundred

feet thick,
of unimagined delicacy.
"Picking periwinkles from the cracks"
or killing prey with the concentric crushing rigor of the python,
it hovers forward "spider fashion
on its arms" misleadingly like lace;
its "ghostly pallor changing
to the green metallic tinge of an anemone-starred pool."
The fir-trees, in "the magnitude of their root systems,"
rise aloof from these maneuvers "creepy to behold,"
austere specimens of our American royal families,
"each like the shadow of the one beside it.
The rock seems frail compared with their dark energy of life,"
its vermilion and onyx and manganese-blue interior expensiveness
left at the mercy of the weather;
"stained transversely by iron where the water drips down,"
recognized by its plants and its animals.
Completing a circle,
you have been deceived into thinking that you have progressed,
under the polite needles of the larches
"hung to filter, not to intercept the sunlight"—
met by tightly wattled spruce-twigs
"conformed to an edge like clipped cypress
as if no branch could penetrate the cold beyond its company";
and dumps of gold and silver ore enclosing The Goat's Mirror—

that lady-fingerlike depression in the shape of the left human
                                                            foot,

which prejudices you in favor of itself
before you have had time to see the others;
its indigo, pea-green, blue-green, and turquoise,
from a hundred to two hundred feet deep,
"merging in irregular patches in the middle lake
where, like gusts of a storm
obliterating the shadows of the fir-trees, the wind makes lanes
                                                            of ripples."
What spot could have merits of equal importance
for bears, elk, deer, wolves, goats, and ducks?
Pre-empted by their ancestors,
this is the property of the exacting porcupine,
and of the rat "slipping along to its burrow in the swamp
or pausing on high ground to smell the heather";
of "thoughtful beavers
making drains which seem the work of careful men with shovels,"
and of the bears inspecting unexpectedly
ant-hills and berry-bushes.
Composed of calcium gems and alabaster pillars,
topaz, tourmaline crystals and amethyst quartz,
their den is somewhere else, concealed in the confusion
of "blue forests thrown together with marble and jasper and agate
as if whole quarries had been dynamited."
And farther up, in stag-at-bay position
as a scintillating fragment of these terrible stalagmites,
stands the goat,
its eye fixed on the waterfall which never seems to fall—
an endless skein swayed by the wind,
immune to force of gravity in the perspective of the peaks.
A special antelope
acclimated to "grottoes from which issue penetrating draughts
which make you wonder why you came,"
it stands its ground
on cliffs the color of the clouds, of petrified white vapor—

black feet, eyes, nose, and horns, engraved on dazzling ice-fields,
the ermine body on the crystal peak;
the sun kindling its shoulders to maximum heat like acetylene,
                                        dyeing them white—
upon this antique pedestal,
"a mountain with those graceful lines which prove it a volcano,"
its top a complete cone like Fujiyama's
till an explosion blew it off.
Distinguished by a beauty
of which "the visitor dare never fully speak at home
for fear of being stoned as an impostor,"
Big Snow Mountain is the home of a diversity of creatures:
those who "have lived in hotels
but who now live in camps—who prefer to";
the mountain guide evolving from the trapper,
"in two pairs of trousers, the outer one older,
wearing slowly away from the feet to the knees";
"the nine-striped chipmunk
running with unmammal-like agility along a log";
the water ouzel
with "its passion for rapids and high-pressured falls,"
building under the arch of some tiny Niagara;
the white-tailed ptarmigan "in winter solid white,
feeding on heather-bells and alpine buckwheat";
and the eleven eagles of the west,
"fond of the spring fragrance and the winter colors,"
used to the unegoistic action of the glaciers
and "several hours of frost every midsummer night."
"They make a nice appearance, don't they,"
happy seeing nothing?
Perched on treacherous lava and pumice—
those unadjusted chimney-pots and cleavers
which stipulate "names and addresses of persons to notify
in case of disaster"—
they hear the roar of ice and supervise the water
winding slowly through the cliffs,

the road "climbing like the thread
which forms the groove around a snail-shell,
doubling back and forth until where snow begins, it ends."
No "deliberate wide-eyed wistfulness" is here
among the boulders sunk in ripples and white water
where "when you hear the best wild music of the forest
it is sure to be a marmot,"
the victim on some slight observatory,
of "a struggle between curiosity and caution,"
inquiring what has scared it:
a stone from the moraine descending in leaps,
another marmot, or the spotted ponies with glass eyes,
brought up on frosty grass and flowers
and rapid draughts of ice-water.
Instructed none knows how, to climb the mountain,
by business men who require for recreation
three hundred and sixty-five holidays in the year,
these conspicuously spotted little horses are peculiar;
hard to discern among the birch-trees, ferns, and lily-pads,
avalanche lilies, Indian paint-brushes,
bear's ears and kittentails,
and miniature cavalcades of chlorophylless fungi
magnified in profile on the moss-beds like moonstones in the water;
the cavalcade of calico competing
with the original American menagerie of styles
among the white flowers of the rhododendron surmounting
                                     rigid leaves
upon which moisture works its alchemy,
transmuting verdure into onyx.

"Like happy souls in Hell," enjoying mental difficulties,
                                     the Greeks
amused themselves with delicate behavior
because it was "so noble and so fair";
not practised in adapting their intelligence
to eagle-traps and snow-shoes,

to alpenstocks and other toys contrived by those
"alive to the advantage of invigorating pleasures."
Bows, arrows, oars, and paddles, for which trees provide the

wood,

in new countries more eloquent than elsewhere—
augmenting the assertion that, essentially humane,
"the forest affords wood for dwellings and by its beauty
stimulates the moral vigor of its citizens."
The Greeks liked smoothness, distrusting what was back
of what could not be clearly seen,
resolving with benevolent conclusiveness,
"complexities which still will be complexities
as long as the world lasts";
ascribing what we clumsily call happiness,
to "an accident or a quality,
a spiritual substance or the soul itself,
an act, a disposition, or a habit,
or a habit infused, to which the soul has been persuaded,
or something distinct from a habit, a power"—
such power as Adam had and we are still devoid of.
"Emotionally sensitive, their hearts were hard";
their wisdom was remote
from that of these odd oracles of cool official sarcasm,
upon this game preserve
where "guns, nets, seines, traps and explosives,
hired vehicles, gambling and intoxicants are prohibited;
disobedient persons being summarily removed
and not allowed to return without permission in writing."
It is self-evident
that it is frightful to have everything afraid of one;
that one must do as one is told
and eat rice, prunes, dates, raisins, hardtack, and tomatoes
if one would "conquer the main peak of Mount Tacoma,
this fossil flower concise without a shiver,
intact when it is cut,
damned for its sacrosanct remoteness—

like Henry James "damned by the public for decorum";
not decorum, but restraint;
it is the love of doing hard things
that rebuffed and wore them out—a public out of sympathy
                                        with neatness.

Neatness of finish! Neatness of finish!
Relentless accuracy is the nature of this octopus
with its capacity for fact.
"Creeping slowly as with meditated stealth,
its arms seeming to approach from all directions,"
it receives one under winds that "tear the snow to bits
and hurl it like a sandblast
shearing off twigs and loose bark from the trees."
Is "tree" the word for these things
"flat on the ground like vines"?
some "bent in a half circle with branches on one side
suggesting dust-brushes, not trees;
some finding strength in union, forming little stunted groves
their flattened mats of branches shrunk in trying to escape"
from the hard mountain "planed by ice and polished by the
                                        wind"—

the white volcano with no weather side;
the lightning flashing at its base,
rain falling in the valleys, and snow falling on the peak—
the glassy octopus symmetrically pointed,
its claw cut by the avalanche
"with a sound like the crack of a rifle,
in a curtain of powdered snow launched like a waterfall."

SEA UNICORNS AND LAND UNICORNS

with their respective lions—
"mighty monoceroses with immeasured tayles"—
these are those very animals
described by the cartographers of 1539,
defiantly revolving
in such a way that
the long keel of white exhibited in tumbling,
disperses giant weeds
and those sea snakes whose forms, looped in the foam, "disquiet
shippers."
Knowing how a voyager obtained the horn of a sea unicorn
to give to Queen Elizabeth,
who thought it worth a hundred thousand pounds,
they persevere in swimming where they like,
finding the place where sea-lions live in herds,
strewn on the beach like stones with lesser stones—
and bears are white;
discovering Antarctica, its penguin kings and icy spires,
and Sir John Hawkins' Florida
"abounding in land unicorns and lions;
since where the one is,
its arch enemy cannot be missing."
Thus personalities by nature much opposed,
can be combined in such a way
that when they do agree, their unanimity is great,
"in politics, in trade, law, sport, religion,
china-collecting, tennis, and church going."
You have remarked this fourfold combination of strange animals,
upon embroideries
enwrought with "polished garlands" of agreeing difference—
thorns, "myrtle rods, and shafts of bay,"
"cobwebs, and knotts, and mulberries"
of lapis-lazuli and pomegranate and malachite—

Britannia's sea unicorn with its rebellious child
now ostentatiously indigenous to the new English coast;
and its land lion oddly tolerant of those pacific counterparts to it,
the water lions of the west.
This is a strange fraternity—these sea lions and land lions,
land unicorns and sea unicorns:
the lion civilly rampant,
tame and concessive like the long-tailed bear of Ecuador—
the lion standing up against this screen of woven air
which is the forest:
the unicorn also, on its hind legs in reciprocity.
A puzzle to the hunters, is this haughtiest of beasts,
to be distinguished from those born without a horn,
in use like Saint Jerome's tame lion, as domestics;
rebelling proudly at the dogs
which are dismayed by the chain lightning
playing at them from its horn—
the dogs persistent in pursuit of it as if it could be caught,
"deriving agreeable terror" from its "moonbeam throat"
on fire like its white coat and unconsumed as if of salamander's
skin.

So wary as to disappear for centuries and reappear,
yet never to be caught,
the unicorn has been preserved
by an unmatched device
wrought like the work of expert blacksmiths—
this animal of that one horn
throwing itself upon which head foremost from a cliff,
it walks away unharmed;
proficient in this feat which, like Herodotus,
I have not seen except in pictures.
Thus this strange animal with its miraculous elusiveness,
has come to be unique,
"impossible to take alive,"
tamed only by a lady inoffensive like itself—
as curiously wild and gentle;

"as straight and slender as the crest,
or antlet of the one-beam'd beast."
Upon the printed page,
also by word of mouth,
we have a record of it all
and how, unfearful of deceit,
etched like an equine monster of an old celestial map,
beside a cloud or dress of Virgin-Mary blue,
improved "all over slightly with shakes of Venice gold,
and silver, and some O's,"
the unicorn "with pavon high," approaches eagerly;
until engrossed by what appears of this strange enemy,
upon the map, "upon her lap,"
its "mild wild head doth lie."

THE MONKEY PUZZLE

A kind of monkey or pine-lemur
not of interest to the monkey,
in a kind of Flaubert's Carthage, it defies one—
this "Paduan cat with lizard," this "tiger in a bamboo thicket."
"An interwoven somewhat," it will not come out.
Ignore the Foo dog and it is forthwith more than a dog,
its tail superimposed upon itself in a complacent half spiral,
this pine-tree—this pine-tiger, is a tiger, not a dog.
It knows that if a nomad may have dignity,
Gibraltar has had more—
that "it is better to be lonely than unhappy."
A conifer contrived in imitation of the glyptic work of jade and
                                   hard-stone cutters,
a true curio in this bypath of curio-collecting,
it is worth its weight in gold, but no one takes it
from these woods in which society's not knowing is colossal,
the lion's ferocious chrysanthemum head seeming kind by
                                   comparison.

This porcupine-quilled, complicated starkness—
this is beauty—"a certain proportion in the skeleton which
                                   gives the best results."
One is at a loss, however, to know why it should be here,
in this morose part of the earth—
to account for its origin at all;
but we prove, we do not explain our birth.

INJUDICIOUS GARDENING

If yellow betokens infidelity,
   I am an infidel.
      I could not bear a yellow rose ill will
      because books said that yellow boded ill,
   white promised well.

However, your particular possession,
   the sense of privacy,
      indeed might deprecate
      offended ears, and need not tolerate
   effrontery.

TO MILITARY PROGRESS

You use your mind
like a millstone to grind
   chaff.
You polish it
and with your warped wit
   laugh

at your torso,
prostrate where the crow
   falls
on such faint hearts
as its god imparts,
   calls

and claps its wings
till the tumult brings
   more
black minute-men
to revive again,
   war

at little cost.
They cry for the lost
   head
and seek their prize
till the evening sky's
   red.

AN EGYPTIAN PULLED GLASS BOTTLE
IN THE SHAPE OF A FISH

Here we have thirst
and patience, from the first,
    and art, as in a wave held up for us to see
    in its essential perpendicularity

not brittle but
intense—the spectrum, that
    spectacular and nimble animal the fish,
    whose scales turn aside the sun's sword by their polish.

TO A STEAM ROLLER

The illustration
is nothing to you without the application.
    You lack half wit. You crush all the particles down
        into close conformity, and then walk back and forth on them.

Sparkling chips of rock
are crushed down to the level of the parent block.
    Were not "impersonal judgment in aesthetic
        matters, a metaphysical impossibility," you

might fairly achieve
it. As for butterflies, I can hardly conceive
    of one's attending upon you, but to question
        the congruence of the complement is vain, if it exists.

TO A SNAIL

If "compression is the first grace of style,"
you have it. Contractility is a virtue
as modesty is a virtue.
It is not the acquisition of any one thing
that is able to adorn,
or the incidental quality that occurs
as a concomitant of something well said,
that we value in style,
but the principle that is hid:
in the absence of feet, "a method of conclusions";
"a knowledge of principles,"
in the curious phenomenon of your occipital horn.

"NOTHING WILL CURE THE SICK LION BUT TO EAT AN APE"

Perceiving that in the masked ball
attitude, there is a hollowness
that beauty's light momentum can't redeem;
   since disproportionate satisfaction anywhere
   lacks a proportionate air,

he let us know without offense
by his hands' denunciatory
upheaval, that he despised the fashion
   of curing us with an ape—making it his care
   to smother us with fresh air.

TO THE PEACOCK OF FRANCE

In "taking charge of your possessions when you saw them" you
                                                    became a golden jay.
Scaramouche said you charmed his charm away,
  but not his color? Yes, his color when you liked.
  Of chiseled setting and black-opalescent dye,
    you were the jewelry of sense;
      of sense, not license; you but trod the pace
      of liberty in market-place
        and court. Molière,
        the huggermugger repertory of your first adventure,
                                                    is your own affair.

"Anchorites do not dwell in theatres," and peacocks do not
                                                    flourish in a cell.
Why make distinctions? The results were well
  when you were on the boards; nor were your triumphs bought
  at horrifying sacrifice of stringency.
    You hated sham; you ranted up
      and down through the conventions of excess;
      nor did the King love you the less
        nor did the world,
        in whose chief interest and for whose spontaneous
                                                    delight, your broad tail was unfurled.

THE PAST IS THE PRESENT

If external action is effete
   and rhyme is outmoded,
     I shall revert to you,
   Habakkuk, as when in a Bible class
     the teacher was speaking of unrhymed verse.
He said—and I think I repeat his exact words,
     "Hebrew poetry is prose
  with a sort of heightened consciousness." Ecstasy affords
     the occasion and expediency determines the form.

"HE WROTE THE HISTORY BOOK"

There! You shed a ray
   of whimsicality on a mask of profundity so
      terrific, that I have been dumbfounded by
it oftener than I care to say.
            The book? Titles are chaff.

Authentically
   brief and full of energy, you contribute to your father's
      legibility and are sufficiently
synthetic. Thank you for showing me
         your father's autograph.

SOJOURN IN THE WHALE

Trying to open locked doors with a sword, threading
   the points of needles, planting shade trees
   upside down; swallowed by the opaqueness of one whom the
                                     seas
love better than they love you, Ireland—

you have lived and lived on every kind of shortage.
   You have been compelled by hags to spin
   gold thread from straw and have heard men say:
"There is a feminine temperament in direct contrast to ours,

which makes her do these things. Circumscribed by a
   heritage of blindness and native
   incompetence, she will become wise and will be forced to give in.
Compelled by experience, she will turn back;

water seeks its own level":
   and you have smiled. "Water in motion is far
   from level." You have seen it, when obstacles happened to bar
the path, rise automatically.

SILENCE

My father used to say,
"Superior people never make long visits,
have to be shown Longfellow's grave
or the glass flowers at Harvard.
Self-reliant like the cat—
that takes its prey to privacy,
the mouse's limp tail hanging like a shoelace from its mouth—
they sometimes enjoy solitude,
and can be robbed of speech
by speech which has delighted them.
The deepest feeling always shows itself in silence;
not in silence, but restraint."
Nor was he insincere in saying, "Make my house your inn."
Inns are not residences.

WHAT ARE YEARS (1941)

WHAT ARE YEARS?

What is our innocence,
what is our guilt? All are
    naked, none is safe. And whence
is courage: the unanswered question,
the resolute doubt,—
dumbly calling, deafly listening—that
in misfortune, even death,
        encourages others
        and in its defeat, stirs

    the soul to be strong? He
sees deep and is glad, who
    accedes to mortality
and in his imprisonment rises
upon himself as
the sea in a chasm, struggling to be
free and unable to be,
        in its surrendering
        finds its continuing.

    So he who strongly feels,
behaves. The very bird,
    grown taller as he sings, steels
his form straight up. Though he is captive,
his mighty singing
says, satisfaction is a lowly
thing, how pure a thing is joy.
        This is mortality,
        this is eternity.

RIGORISTS

"We saw reindeer
browsing," a friend who'd been in Lapland, said:
"finding their own food; they are adapted

to scant *reino*
or pasture, yet they can run eleven
miles in fifty minutes; the feet spread when

the snow is soft,
and act as snow-shoes. They are rigorists,
however handsomely cutwork artists

of Lapland and
Siberia elaborate the trace
or saddle-girth with saw-tooth leather lace.

One looked at us
with its firm face part brown, part white—a queen
of alpine flowers. Santa Claus' reindeer, seen

at last, had gray-
brown fur, with a neck like edelweiss or
lion's foot—*leontopodium* more

exactly." And
this candelabrum-headed ornament
for a place where ornaments are scarce, sent

to Alaska,
was a gift preventing the extinction
of the Eskimo. The battle was won

by a quiet man,
Sheldon Jackson, evangel to that race
whose reprieve he read in the reindeer's face.

LIGHT IS SPEECH

One can say more of sunlight
    than of speech; but speech
    and light, each
aiding each—when French—
have not disgraced that still
unextirpated adjective.
Yes, light is speech. Free frank
impartial sunlight, moonlight,
starlight, lighthouse light,
    are language. The Creach'h
d'Ouessant light-
house on its defenseless dot of
rock, is the descendant of Voltaire

whose flaming justice reached
    a man already harmed;
    of unarmed
Montaigne whose balance,
maintained despite the bandit's
hardness, lit remorse's saving
spark; of Émile Littré,
philology's determined,
ardent eight-volume
    Hippocrates-charmed
editor. A
man of fire, a scientist of
freedoms, was firm Maximilien

Paul Émile Littré. England
    guarded by the sea,
    we, with re-enforced Bartholdi's
Liberty holding up her
torch beside the port, hear France
demand, "Tell me the truth,

especially when it is
     unpleasant." And we
cannot but reply,
"The word France means
enfranchisement; means one who can
'animate whoever thinks of her.'"

HE "DIGESTETH HARDE YRON"

Although the aepyornis
or roc that lived in Madagascar, and
the moa are extinct,
the camel-sparrow, linked
with them in size—the large sparrow
Xenophon saw walking by a stream—was and is
a symbol of justice.

This bird watches his chicks with
a maternal concentration—and he's
been mothering the eggs
at night six weeks—his legs
their only weapon of defense.
He is swifter than a horse; he has a foot hard
as a hoof; the leopard

is not more suspicious. How
could he, prized for plumes and eggs and young,
used even as a riding-beast, respect men
hiding actor-like in ostrich skins, with the right hand
making the neck move as if alive
and from a bag the left hand strewing grain, that ostriches

might be decoyed and killed! Yes, this is he
whose plume was anciently
the plume of justice; he
whose comic duckling head on its
great neck revolves with compass-needle nervousness
when he stands guard,

in S-like foragings as he is
preening the down on his leaden-skinned back.

The egg piously shown
as Leda's very own
    from which Castor and Pollux hatched,
was an ostrich-egg. And what could have been more fit
for the Chinese lawn it

    grazed on as a gift to an
    emperor who admired strange birds, than this
one, who builds his mud-made
nest in dust yet will wade
    in lake or sea till only the head shows.

                .   .   .

    Six hundred ostrich-brains served
    at one banquet, the ostrich-plume-tipped tent
and desert spear, jewel-
gorgeous ugly egg-shell
    goblets, eight pairs of ostriches
in harness, dramatize a meaning
always missed by the externalist.

    The power of the visible
    is the invisible; as even where
no tree of freedom grows,
so-called brute courage knows.
    Heroism is exhausting, yet
it contradicts a greed that did not wisely spare
the harmless solitaire

    or great auk in its grandeur;
    unsolicitude having swallowed up
all giant birds but an alert gargantuan
    little-winged, magnificently speedy running-bird.
This one remaining rebel
is the sparrow-camel.

THE STUDENT

"In America," began
the lecturer, "everyone must have a
degree. The French do not think that
all can have it, they don't say everyone
        must go to college." We
incline to feel, here,
        that although it may be unnecessary

to know fifteen languages,
one degree is not too much. With us, a
school—like the singing tree of which
the leaves were mouths that sang in concert—
        is both a tree of knowledge
and of liberty,—
        seen in the unanimity of college

mottoes, *lux et veritas*,
Christo et ecclesiae, sapiet
felici. It may be that we
have not knowledge, just opinions, that we
    are undergraduates,
not students; we know
    we have been told with smiles, by expatriates

of whom we had asked "When will
your experiment be finished?" "Science
is never finished." Secluded
from domestic strife, Jack Bookworm led a
    college life, says Goldsmith;
and here also as
    in France or Oxford, study is beset with

dangers—with bookworms, mildews,
and complaisancies. But someone in New
England has known enough to say
that the student is patience personified,
    a variety
of hero, "patient
    of neglect and of reproach,"—who can "hold by

himself." You can't beat hens to
make them lay. Wolf's wool is the best of wool,
but it cannot be sheared, because
the wolf will not comply. With knowledge as
    with wolves' surliness,
the student studies
    voluntarily, refusing to be less

than individual. He
"gives his opinion and then rests upon it";
he renders service when there is
no reward, and is too reclusive for
    some things to seem to touch
him; not because he
    has no feeling but because he has so much.

SMOOTH GNARLED CRAPE MYRTLE

A brass-green bird with grass-
green throat smooth as a nut springs from
    twig to twig askew, copying the
Chinese flower piece—businesslike atom
    in the stiff-leafed tree's blue-
    pink dregs-of-wine pyramids
    of mathematic
    circularity; one of a
    pair. A redbird with a hatchet
    crest lights straight, on a twig
    between the two, bending the
        peculiar
        bouquet down; and there are

    moths and lady-bugs,
a boot-jack firefly with black wings
    and a pink head. "The legendary white-
eared black bulbul that sings
    only in pure Sanskrit" should
    be here—"tame clever
    true nightingale." The cardinal-
    bird that is usually a
    pair, looks somewhat odd, like
    "the ambassadorial
        Inverness
        worn by one who dresses

    in New York but dreams of
London." It was artifice saw,
    on a patch-box pigeon-egg, room for
fervent script, and wrote as with a bird's claw
    under the pair on the
    hyacinth-blue lid—"joined in

friendship, crowned by love."
An aspect may deceive; as the
elephant's columbine-tubed trunk
held waveringly out—
an at will heavy thing—is
delicate.
Art is unfortunate.

One may be a blameless
bachelor, and it is but a step
to Congreve. A Rosalindless
redbird comes where people are, knowing they
have not made a point of
being where he is—this bird
which says not sings, "without
loneliness I should be more
lonely, so I keep it"—half in
Japanese. And what of
our clasped hands that swear, "By Peace
Plenty; as
by Wisdom Peace." Alas!

BIRD-WITTED

With innocent wide penguin eyes, three
   large fledgling mocking-birds below
the pussy-willow tree,
   stand in a row,
wings touching, feebly solemn,
till they see
     their no longer larger
     mother bringing
something which will partially
feed one of them.

Toward the high-keyed intermittent squeak
   of broken carriage-springs, made by
the three similar, meek-
   coated bird's-eye
freckled forms she comes; and when
from the beak
     of one, the still living
     beetle has dropped
out, she picks it up and puts
it in again.

Standing in the shade till they have dressed
   their thickly-filamented, pale
pussy-willow-surfaced
   coats, they spread tail
and wings, showing one by one,
the modest
     white stripe lengthwise on the
     tail and crosswise
underneath the wing, and the
accordion

is closed again. What delightful note
   with rapid unexpected flute-
sounds leaping from the throat
   of the astute
grown bird, comes back to one from
the remote
      unenergetic sun-
      lit air before
the brood was here? How harsh
the bird's voice has become.

A piebald cat observing them,
   is slowly creeping toward the trim
trio on the tree-stem.
   Unused to him
the three make room—uneasy
new problem.
      A dangling foot that missed
      its grasp, is raised
and finds the twig on which it
planned to perch. The

parent darting down, nerved by what chills
   the blood, and by hope rewarded—
of toil—since nothing fills
   squeaking unfed
mouths, wages deadly combat,
and half kills
      with bayonet beak and
      cruel wings, the
intellectual cautious-
ly c r e e p ing cat.

VIRGINIA BRITANNIA

Pale sand edges England's Old
Dominion. The air is soft, warm, hot
above the cedar-dotted emerald shore
     known to the red-bird, the red-coated musketeer,
     the trumpet-flower, the cavalier,
     the parson, and the wild parishioner. A deer-
track in a church-floor
     brick, and a fine pavement tomb with engraved top, remain.
     The now tremendous vine-encompassed hackberry
          starred with the ivy-flower,
          shades the tall tower;
And a great sinner lyeth here under the sycamore.

A fritillary zigzags
toward the chancel-shaded resting-place
of this unusual man and sinner who
     waits for a joyful resurrection. We-re-wo-
     co-mo-co's fur crown could be no
     odder than we were, with ostrich, Latin motto,
and small gold horse-shoe:
     arms for an able sting-ray-hampered pioneer—
     painted as a Turk, it seems—continuously
          exciting Captain Smith
          who, patient with
his inferiors, was a pugnacious equal, and to

Powhatan as unflattering
as grateful. Rare Indian, crowned by
Christopher Newport! The Old Dominion has
     all-green box-sculptured grounds.
     An almost English green surrounds
     them. Care has formed among unEnglish insect sounds,
the white wall-rose. As

thick as Daniel Boone's grape-vine, the stem has wide-spaced
                                                      great

blunt alternating ostrich-skin warts that were thorns.
    Care has formed walls of yew
    since Indians knew
the Fort Old Field and narrow tongue of land that Jamestown
                                                    was.

Observe the terse Virginian,
    the mettlesome gray one that drives the
owl from tree to tree and imitates the call
        of whippoorwill or lark or katydid—the lead-
        gray lead-legged mocking-bird with head
        held half away, and meditative eye as dead
as sculptured marble
    eye, alighting noiseless, musing in the semi-sun,
    standing on tall thin legs as if he did not see,
        conspicuous, alone,
        on the stone-
topped table with lead cupids grouped to form the pedestal.

Narrow herring-bone-laid bricks,
    a dusty pink beside the dwarf box-
bordered pansies, share the ivy-arbor shade
        with cemetery lace settees, one at each side,
        and with the bird: box-bordered tide-
        water gigantic jet black pansies—splendor; pride—
not for a decade
    dressed, but for a day, in over-powering velvet; and
    gray-blue-Andalusian-cock-feather pale ones,
        ink-lined on the edge, fur-
        eyed, with ochre
on the cheek. The at first slow, saddle-horse quick cavalcade

    of buckeye-burnished jumpers
    and five-gaited mounts, the work-mule and

show-mule and witch-cross door and "strong sweet prison"
      are a part of what has come about—in the Black
      idiom—from "advancin' back-
      wards in a circle"; from taking the Potomac
cowbirdlike, and on
      the Chickahominy establishing the Negro,
      inadvertent ally and best enemy of
            tyranny. Rare unscent-
            ed, provident-
ly hot, too sweet, inconsistent flower-bed! Old Dominion

      flowers are curious. Some wilt
      in daytime and some close at night. Some
have perfume; some have not. The scarlet much-quilled
      fruiting pomegranate, the African violet,
      fuchsia and camellia, none; yet
      the house-high glistening green magnolia's velvet-
textured flower is filled
      with anesthetic scent as inconsiderate as
      the gardenia's. Even the gardenia-sprig's
            dark vein on greener
            leaf when seen
against the light, has not near it more small bees than the
                                                    frilled

      silk substanceless faint flower of
      the crape-myrtle has. Odd Pamunkey
princess, birdclaw-ear-ringed; with a pet raccoon
      from the Mattaponi (what a bear!). Feminine
      odd Indian young lady! Odd thin-
      gauze-and-taffeta-dressed English one! Terrapin
meat and crested spoon
      feed the mistress of French plum-and-turquoise-piped
                                                    chaise-longue;
      of brass-knobbed slat front door, and everywhere open
            shaded house on Indian-

named Virginian
streams in counties named for English lords. The rattlesnake
soon

said from our once dashingly
undiffident first flag, "Don't tread on
me"—tactless symbol of a new republic.
Priorities were cradled in this region not
noted for humility; spot
that has high-singing frogs, cotton-mouth snakes and cot-
ton-fields; a unique
Lawrence pottery with loping wolf design; and too
unvenomous terrapin in tepid greenness,
idling near the sea-top;
tobacco-crop
records on church walls; a Devil's Woodyard; and the one-brick-

thick serpentine wall built by
Jefferson. Like strangler figs choking
a banyan, not an explorer, no imperialist,
not one of us, in taking what we
pleased—in colonizing as the
saying is—has been a synonym for mercy.
The redskin with the deer-
fur crown, famous for his cruelty, is not all brawn
and animality. The outdoor tea-table,
the mandolin-shaped big
and little fig,
the silkworm-mulberry, the French mull dress with the
Madeira-

vine-accompanied edge are,
when compared with what the colonists
found here in tidewater Virginia, stark
luxuries. The mere brown hedge-sparrow, with reckless
ardor, unable to suppress

his satisfaction in man's trustworthy nearness,
even in the dark
   flutes his ecstatic burst of joy—the caraway seed-
   spotted sparrow perched in the dew-drenched juniper
      beside the window-ledge;
      this little hedge-
sparrow that wakes up seven minutes sooner than the lark.

   The live oak's darkening filigree
   of undulating boughs, the etched
solidity of a cypress indivisible
      from the now agèd English hackberry,
      become with lost identity,
      part of the ground, as sunset flames increasingly
against the leaf-chiseled
   blackening ridge of green; while clouds, expanding àbove
   the town's assertiveness, dwarf it, dwarf arrogance
      that can misunderstand
      importance; and
are to the child an intimation of what glory is.

has not altered;—
   a place as kind as it is green,
   the greenest place I've never seen.
Every name is a tune.
Denunciations do not affect
     the culprit; nor blows, but it
is torture to him to not be spoken to.
They're natural,—
      the coat, like Venus'
mantle lined with stars,
buttoned close at the neck,—the sleeves new from disuse.

If in Ireland
   they play the harp backward at need,
   and gather at midday the seed
of the fern, eluding
their "giants all covered with iron," might
     there be fern seed for unlearn-
ing obduracy and for reinstating
the enchantment?
      Hindered characters
seldom have mothers
in Irish stories, but they all have grandmothers.

It was Irish;
   a match not a marriage was made
   when my great great grandmother'd said
with native genius for
disunion, "Although your suitor be
     perfection, one objection
is enough; he is not

Irish." Outwitting
          the fairies, befriending the furies,
whoever again
and again says, "I'll never give in," never sees

that you're not free
    until you've been made captive by
    supreme belief,—credulity
you say? When large dainty
fingers tremblingly divide the wings
        of the fly for mid-July
with a needle and wrap it with peacock-tail,
or tie wool and
          buzzard's wing, their pride,
like the enchanter's
is in care, not madness. Concurring hands divide

flax for damask
    that when bleached by Irish weather
    has the silvered chamois-leather
water-tightness of a
skin. Twisted torcs and gold new-moon-shaped
        lunulae aren't jewelry
like the purple-coral fuchsia-tree's. Eire—
the guillemot
          so neat and the hen
of the heath and the
linnet spinet-sweet—bespeak relentlessness? Then

they are to me
    like enchanted Earl Gerald who
    changed himself into a stag, to
a great green-eyed cat of
the mountain. Discommodity makes

them invisible; they've dis-
appeared. The Irish say your trouble is their
trouble and your
          joy their joy? I wish
I could believe it;
I am troubled, I'm dissatisfied, I'm Irish.

FOUR QUARTZ CRYSTAL CLOCKS

There are four vibrators, the world's exactest clocks;
   and these quartz time-pieces that tell
time intervals to other clocks,
   these workless clocks work well;
independently the same, kept in
   the 41° Bell
     Laboratory time

vault. Checked by a comparator with Arlington,
   they punctualize the "radio,
cinéma," and "presse,"—a group the
   Giraudoux truth-bureau
of hoped-for accuracy has termed
   "instruments of truth." We know—
     as Jean Giraudoux says,

certain Arabs have not heard—that Napoleon
   is dead; that a quartz prism when
the temperature changes, feels
   the change and that the then
electrified alternate edges
   oppositely charged, threaten
     careful timing; so that

this water-clear crystal as the Greeks used to say,
   this "clear ice" must be kept at the
same coolness. Repetition, with
   the scientist, should be
synonymous with accuracy.
   The lemur-student can see
     that an aye-aye is not

an angwan-tíbo, potto, or loris. The sea-
   side burden should not embarrass
the bell-boy with the buoy-ball
   endeavoring to pass
hotel patronesses; nor could a
   practiced ear confuse the glass
      eyes for taxidermists

with eye-glasses from the optometrist. And as
   MEridian-7 one-two
one-two gives, each fifteenth second
   in the same voice, the new
data—"The time will be" so and so—
   you realize that "when you
      hear the signal," you'll be

hearing Jupiter or jour pater, the day god—
   the salvaged son of Father Time—
telling the cannibal Chronos
   (eater of his proxime
newborn progeny) that punctuality
   is not a crime.

THE PANGOLIN

Another armored animal—scale
    lapping scale with spruce-cone regularity until they
form the uninterrupted central
    tail-row! This near artichoke with head and legs and
                            grit-equipped gizzard,
    the night miniature artist engineer is,
        yes, Leonardo da Vinci's replica—
        impressive animal and toiler of whom we seldom hear.
    Armor seems extra. But for him,
        the closing ear-ridge—
            or bare ear lacking even this small
            eminence and similarly safe

contracting nose and eye apertures
    impenetrably closable, are not; —a true ant-eater,
not cockroach-eater, who endures
    exhausting solitary trips through unfamiliar ground at night,
    returning before sunrise; stepping in the moonlight,
        on the moonlight peculiarly, that the outside
           edges of his hands may bear the weight and save the
                          claws
        for digging. Serpentined about
           the tree, he draws
           away from danger unpugnaciously,
           with no sound but a harmless hiss; keeping

the fragile grace of the Thomas-
    of-Leighton Buzzard Westminster Abbey wrought-iron
                              vine, or
rolls himself into a ball that has
    power to defy all effort to unroll it; strongly intailed, neat
    head for core, on neck not breaking off, with curled-in feet.
        Nevertheless he has sting-proof scales; and nest

of rocks closed with earth from inside, which he can
thus darken.
Sun and moon and day and night and man and beast
each with a splendor
which man in all his vileness cannot
set aside; each with an excellence!

"Fearful yet to be feared," the armored
ant-eater met by the driver-ant does not turn back, but
engulfs what he can, the flattened sword-
edged leafpoints on the tail and artichoke set leg- and
body-plates
quivering violently when it retaliates
and swarms on him. Compact like the furled fringed frill
on the hat-brim of Gargallo's hollow iron head of a
matador, he will drop and will
then walk away
unhurt, although if unintruded on,
he cautiously works down the tree, helped

by his tail. The giant-pangolin-
tail, graceful tool, as prop or hand or broom or ax, tipped like
an elephant's trunk with special skin,
is not lost on this ant- and stone-swallowing uninjurable
artichoke which simpletons thought a living fable
whom the stones had nourished, whereas ants had done
so. Pangolins are not aggressive animals; between
dusk and day they have the not unchain-like machine-like
form and frictionless creep of a thing
made graceful by adversities, con-

versities. To explain grace requires
a curious hand. If that which is at all were not forever,
why would those who graced the spires

with animals and gathered there to rest, on cold luxurious
low stone seats—a monk and monk and monk—between the
thus
ingenious roof-supports, have slaved to confuse
grace with a kindly manner, time in which to pay a
debt,
the cure for sins, a graceful use
of what are yet
approved stone mullions branching out across
the perpendiculars? A sailboat

was the first machine. Pangolins, made
for moving quietly also, are models of exactness,
on four legs; on hind feet plantigrade,
with certain postures of a man. Beneath sun and moon,
man slaving
to make his life more sweet, leaves half the flowers worth
having,
needing to choose wisely how to use his strength;
a paper-maker like the wasp; a tractor of foodstuffs,
like the ant; spidering a length
of web from bluffs
above a stream; in fighting, mechanicked
like the pangolin; capsizing in

disheartenment. Bedizened or stark
naked, man, the self, the being we call human, writing-
master to this world, griffons a dark
"Like does not like like that is obnoxious"; and writes error
with four
r's. Among animals, *one* has a sense of humor.
Humor saves a few steps, it saves years. Unignorant,
modest and unemotional, and all emotion,
he has everlasting vigor,
power to grow,

though there are few creatures who can make one
breathe faster and make one erecter.

Not afraid of anything is he,
      and then goes cowering forth, tread paced to meet an obstacle
at every step. Consistent with the
   formula—warm blood, no gills, two pairs of hands and a few
                                          hairs—that
is a mammal; there he sits in his own habitat,
      serge-clad, strong-shod. The prey of fear, he, always
         curtailed, extinguished, thwarted by the dusk, work
                                          partly done,
      says to the alternating blaze,
         "Again the sun!
            anew each day; and new and new and new,
            that comes into and steadies my soul."

THE PAPER NAUTILUS

For authorities whose hopes
are shaped by mercenaries?
    Writers entrapped by
    teatime fame and by
commuters' comforts? Not for these
    the paper nautilus
    constructs her thin glass shell.

Giving her perishable
souvenir of hope, a dull
    white outside and smooth-
    edged inner surface
glossy as the sea, the watchful
    maker of it guards it
    day and night; she scarcely

eats until the eggs are hatched.
Buried eight-fold in her eight
    arms, for she is in
    a sense a devil-
fish, her glass ram'shorn-cradled freight
    is hid but is not crushed;
    as Hercules, bitten

by a crab loyal to the hydra,
was hindered to succeed,
    the intensively
    watched eggs coming from
the shell free it when they are freed, —

leaving its wasp-nest flaws
of white on white, and close-

laid Ionic chiton-folds
like the lines in the mane of
    a Parthenon horse,
    round which the arms had
wound themselves as if they knew love
    is the only fortress
    strong enough to trust to.

NEVERTHELESS (1944)

NEVERTHELESS

you've seen a strawberry
    that's had a struggle; yet
    was, where the fragments met,

a hedgehog or a star-
    fish for the multitude
    of seeds. What better food

than apple-seeds—the fruit
    within the fruit—locked in
    like counter-curved twin

hazel-nuts? Frost that kills
    the little rubber-plant-
    leaves of *kok-saghyz*-stalks, can't

harm the roots; they still grow
    in frozen ground. Once where
    there was a prickly-pear-

leaf clinging to barbed wire,
    a root shot down to grow
    in earth two feet below;

as carrots form mandrakes
    or a ram's-horn root some-
    times. Victory won't come

to me unless I go
    to it; a grape-tendril
    ties a knot in knots till

knotted thirty times,—so
    the bound twig that's under-
    gone and over-gone, can't stir.

The weak overcomes its
    menace, the strong over-
    comes itself. What is there

like fortitude! What sap
    went through that little thread
    to make the cherry red!

THE WOOD-WEASEL

emerges daintily, the skunk—
don't laugh—in sylvan black and white chipmunk
regalia. The inky thing
adaptively whited with glistening
goat-fur, is wood-warden. In his
ermined well-cuttlefish-inked wool, he is
determination's totem. Out-
lawed? His sweet face and powerful feet go about
in chieftain's coat of Chilcat cloth.
He is his own protection from the moth,

noble little warrior. That
otter-skin on it, the living pole-cat,
smothers anything that stings. Well,—
this same weasel's playful and his weasel
associates are too. Only
Wood-weasels shall associate with me.

ELEPHANTS

Uplifted and waved till immobilized
wistaria-like, the opposing opposed
mouse-gray twined proboscises' trunk formed by two
trunks, fights itself to a spiraled inter-nosed

deadlock of dyke-enforced massiveness. It's a
knock-down drag-out fight that asks no quarter? Just
a pastime, as when the trunk rains on itself
the pool it siphoned up; or when—since each must

provide his forty-pound bough dinner—he broke
the leafy branches. These templars of the Tooth,
these matched intensities, take master care of
master tools. One, sleeping with the calm of youth,

at full length in the half-dry sun-flecked stream-bed,
rests his hunting-horn-curled trunk on shallowed stone.
The sloping hollow of the sleeper's body
cradles the gently breathing eminence's prone

mahout, asleep like a lifeless six-foot
frog, so feather light the elephant's stiff
ear's unconscious of the crossed feet's weight. And the
defenseless human thing sleeps as sound as if

incised with hard wrinkles, embossed with wide ears,
invincibly tusked, made safe by magic hairs!
As if, as if, it is all ifs; we are at
much unease. But magic's masterpiece is theirs—

Houdini's serenity quelling his fears.
Elephant-ear-witnesses-to-be of hymns

and glorias, these ministrants all gray or
gray with white on legs or trunk, are a pilgrims'

pattern of revery not reverence—a
religious procession without any priests,
the centuries-old carefullest unrehearsed
play. Blessed by Buddha's Tooth, the obedient beasts

themselves as toothed temples blessing the street, see
the white elephant carry the cushion that
carries the casket that carries the Tooth.
Amenable to what, matched with him, are gnat

trustees, he does not step on them as the white-
canopied blue-cushioned Tooth is augustly
and slowly returned to the shrine. Though white is
the color of worship and of mourning, he

is not here to worship and he is too wise
to mourn—a life prisoner but reconciled.
With trunk tucked up compactly—the elephant's
sign of defeat—he resisted, but is the child

of reason now. His straight trunk seems to say: when
what we hoped for came to nothing, we revived.
As loss could not ever alter Socrates'
tranquillity, equanimity's contrived

by the elephant. With the Socrates of
animals as with Sophocles the Bee, on whose
tombstone a hive was incised, sweetness tinctures
his gravity. His held-up fore-leg for use

as a stair, to be climbed or descended with
the aid of his ear, expounds the brotherhood

of creatures to man the encroacher, by the
small word with the dot, meaning know—the verb búd.

These knowers "arouse the feeling that they are
allied to man" and can change roles with their trustees.
Hardship makes the soldier; then teachableness
makes him the philosopher—as Socrates,

prudently testing the suspicious thing, knew
the wisest is he who's not sure that he knows.
Who rides on a tiger can never dismount;
asleep on an elephant, that is repose.

A CARRIAGE FROM SWEDEN

They say there is a sweeter air
    where it was made, than we have here;
      a Hamlet's castle atmosphere.
At all events there is in Brooklyn
something that makes me feel at home.

No one may see this put-away
    museum-piece, this country cart
      that inner happiness made art;
and yet, in this city of freckled
integrity it is a vein

of resined straightness from north-wind
    hardened Sweden's once-opposed-to-
      compromise archipelago
of rocks. Washington and Gustavus
Adolphus, forgive our decay.

Seats, dashboard and sides of smooth gourd-
    rind texture, a flowered step, swan-
      dart brake, and swirling crustacean-
tailed equine amphibious creatures
that garnish the axle-tree! What

a fine thing! What unannoying
    romance! And how beautiful, she
      with the natural stoop of the
snowy egret, gray-eyed and straight-haired,
for whom it should come to the door—

of whom it reminds me. The split
    pine fair hair, steady gannet-clear
      eyes and the pine-needled-path deer-

swift step; that is Sweden, land of the
free and the soil for a spruce-tree—

vertical though a seedling—all
        needles: from a green trunk, green shelf
        on shelf fanning out by itself.
The deft white-stockinged dance in thick-soled
shoes! Denmark's sanctuaried Jews!

The puzzle-jugs and hand-spun rugs,
        the root-legged kracken shaped like dogs,
        the hanging buttons and the frogs
that edge the Sunday jackets! Sweden,
you have a runner called the Deer, who

when he's won a race, likes to run
        more; you have the sun-right gable-
        ends due east and west, the table
spread as for a banquet; and the put-
in twin vest-pleats with a fish-fin

effect when you need none. Sweden,
        what makes the people dress that way
        and those who see you wish to stay?
The runner, not too tired to run more
at the end of the race? And that

cart, dolphin-graceful? A Dalén
        light-house, self-lit?—responsive and
        responsible. I understand;
it's not pine-needle-paths that give spring
when they're run on, it's a Sweden

of moated white castles—the bed
        of white flowers densely grown in an S

meaning Sweden and stalwartness,
skill, and a surface that says
Made in Sweden: carts are my trade.

THE MIND IS AN ENCHANTING THING

is an enchanted thing
    like the glaze on a
katydid-wing
        subdivided by sun
        till the nettings are legion.
Like Gieseking playing Scarlatti;

like the apteryx-awl
    as a beak, or the
kiwi's rain-shawl
        of haired feathers, the mind
        feeling its way as though blind,
walks along with its eyes on the ground.

It has memory's ear
    that can hear without
having to hear.
        Like the gyroscope's fall,
        truly unequivocal
because trued by regnant certainty,

it is a power of
    strong enchantment. It
is like the dove-
        neck animated by
        sun; it is memory's eye;
it's conscientious inconsistency.

It tears off the veil; tears
    the temptation, the
mist the heart wears,
        from its eyes—if the heart

has a face; it takes apart
dejection. It's fire in the dove-neck's

iridescence; in the
    inconsistencies
of Scàrlatti.
      Unconfusion submits
      its confusion to proof; it's
not a Herod's oath that cannot change.

IN DISTRUST OF MERITS

Strengthened to live, strengthened to die for
    medals and positioned victories?
They're fighting, fighting, fighting the blind
    man who thinks he sees,—
who cannot see that the enslaver is
enslaved; the hater, harmed. O shining O
      firm star, O tumultuous
         ocean lashed till small things go
      as they will, the mountainous
        wave makes us who look, know

depth. Lost at sea before they fought! O
    star of David, star of Bethlehem,
O black imperial lion
    of the Lord—emblem
of a risen world—be joined at last, be
joined. There is hate's crown beneath which all is
      death; there's love's without which none
        is king; the blessed deeds bless
      the halo. As contagion
        of sickness makes sickness,

contagion of trust can make trust. They're
    fighting in deserts and caves, one by
one, in battalions and squadrons;
    they're fighting that I
may yet recover from the disease, My
Self; some have it lightly; some will die. "Man's
      wolf to man" and we devour
        ourselves. The enemy could not
      have made a greater breach in our
        defenses. One pilot-

ing a blind man can escape him, but
        Job disheartened by false comfort knew
that nothing can be so defeating
        as a blind man who
can see. O alive who are dead, who are
proud not to see, O small dust of the earth
                that walks so arrogantly,
                        trust begets power and faith is
                an affectionate thing. We
                        vow, we make this promise

to the fighting—it's a promise—"We'll
        never hate black, white, red, yellow, Jew,
Gentile, Untouchable." We are
        not competent to
make our vows. With set jaw they are fighting,
fighting, fighting,—some we love whom we know,
                some we love but know not—that
                        hearts may feel and not be numb.
                It cures me; or am I what
                        I can't believe in? Some

in snow, some on crags, some in quicksands,
        little by little, much by much, they
are fighting fighting fighting that where
        there was death there may
be life. "When a man is prey to anger,
he is moved by outside things; when he holds
                his ground in patience patience
                        patience, that is action or
                beauty," the soldier's defense
                and hardest armor for

the fight. The world's an orphans' home. Shall
        we never have peace without sorrow?

without pleas of the dying for
    help that won't come? O
quiet form upon the dust, I cannot
look and yet I must. If these great patient
        dyings—all these agonies
            and wound bearings and bloodshed—
      can teach us how to live, these
          dyings were not wasted.

Hate-hardened heart, O heart of iron,
    iron is iron till it is rust.
There never was a war that was
    not inward; I must
fight till I have conquered in myself what
causes war, but I would not believe it.
        I inwardly did nothing.
           O Iscariot-like crime!
        Beauty is everlasting
          and dust is for a time.

COLLECTED LATER (1951)

A FACE

"I am not treacherous, callous, jealous, superstitious,
superstitious, venomous, or absolutely hideous":
    studying and studying its expression,
    exasperated desperation
        though at no real impasse,
        would gladly break the mirror;

when love of order, ardor, uncircuitous simplicity
with an expression of inquiry, are all one needs to be!
    Certain faces, a few, one or two—or one
    face photographed by recollection—
        to my mind, to my sight,
        must remain a delight.

BY DISPOSITION OF ANGELS

Messengers much like ourselves? Explain it.
Steadfastness the darkness makes explicit?
Something heard most clearly when not near it?
    Above particularities,
these unparticularities praise cannot violate.
  One has seen, in such steadiness never deflected,
  how by darkness a star is perfected.

Star that does not ask me if I see it?
Fir that would not wish me to uproot it?
Speech that does not ask me if I hear it?
    Mysteries expound mysteries.
Steadier than steady, star dazzling me, live and elate,
  no need to say, how like some we have known; too like her,
  too like him, and a-quiver forever.

THE ICOSASPHERE

"In Buckinghamshire hedgerows
   the birds nesting in the merged green density,
      weave little bits of string and moths and feathers and
                       thistledown,
       in parabolic concentric curves" and,
   working for concavity, leave spherical feats of rare efficiency;
   whereas through lack of integration,

avid for someone's fortune,
   three were slain and ten committed perjury,
      six died, two killed themselves, and two paid fines for
                     risks they'd run.
      But then there is the icosasphere
   in which at last we have steel-cutting at its summit of
                     economy,
    since twenty triangles conjoined, can wrap one

ball or double-rounded shell
   with almost no waste, so geometrically
      neat, it's an icosahedron. Would the engineers making one,
      or Mr. J. O. Jackson tell us
   how the Egyptians could have set up seventy-eight-foot solid
                   granite vertically?
   We should like to know how that was done.

HIS SHIELD

The pin-swin or spine-swine
    (the edgehog miscalled hedgehog) with all his edges out,
  echidna and echinoderm in distressed-
pin-cushion thorn-fur coats, the spiny pig or porcupine,
    the rhino with horned snout—
  everything is battle-dressed.

Pig-fur won't do, I'll wrap
    myself in salamander-skin like Presbyter John.
  A lizard in the midst of flames, a firebrand
that is life, asbestos-eyed asbestos-eared, with tattooed nap
    and permanent pig on
  the instep; he can withstand

fire and won't drown. In his
    unconquerable country of unpompous gusto,
  gold was so common none considered it; greed
and flattery were unknown. Though rubies large as tennis-
    balls conjoined in streams so
  that the mountain seemed to bleed,

the inextinguishable
    salamander styled himself but presbyter. His shield
  was his humility. In Carpasian
linen coat, flanked by his household lion-cubs and sable
    retinue, he revealed
  a formula safer than

an armorer's: the power of relinquishing
    what one would keep; that is freedom. Become dinosaur-
  skulled, quilled or salamander-wooled, more ironshod
and javelin-dressed than a hedgehog battalion of steel, but be
    dull. Don't be envied or
  armed with a measuring-rod.

"KEEPING THEIR WORLD LARGE"

All too literally, their flesh and their spirit are our shield.
New York Times, *June 7, 1944*

I should like to see that country's tiles, bedrooms,
stone patios
      and ancient wells: Rinaldo
Caramonica's the cobbler's, Frank Sblendorio's
    and Dominick Angelastro's country—
      the grocer's, the iceman's, the dancer's—the
beautiful Miss Damiano's; wisdom's

    and all angels' Italy, this Christmas Day
this Christmas year.
      A noiseless piano, an
innocent war, the heart that can act against itself. Here,
      each unlike and all alike, could
      so many—stumbling, falling, multiplied
till bodies lay as ground to walk on—

    "If Christ and the apostles died in vain,
I'll die in vain with them"
      against this way of victory.
That forest of white crosses!
    My eyes won't close to it.

    All laid like animals for sacrifice—
like Isaac on the mount,
      were their own sacrifice.

    Marching to death, marching to life?
"Keeping their world large,"
      whose spirits and whose bodies
all too literally were our shield,
    are still our shield.

They fought the enemy,
we fight fat living and self-pity.
        Shine, o shine,
unfalsifying sun, on this sick scene.

EFFORTS OF AFFECTION

Genesis tells us of Jubal and Jabal.
One handled the harp and one herded the cattle.

Unhackneyed Shakespeare's
"hay, sweet hay, which hath no fellow,"
love's extraordinary-ordinary stubbornness
like La Fontaine's done
by each as if by each alone,
smiling and stemming distraction;
      how welcome:

vermin-proof and pilfer-proof integration
in which unself-righteousness humbles inspection.

"You know I'm not a saint!" Sainted obsession.
The bleeding-heart's—that strange rubber fern's attraction

puts perfume to shame.
Unsheared sprays of elephant-ears
do not make a selfish end look like a noble one.
Truly as the sun
can rot or mend, love can make one
bestial or make a beast a man.
      Thus wholeness—

wholesomeness? say efforts of affection—
attain integration too tough for infraction.

VORACITIES AND VERITIES
SOMETIMES ARE INTERACTING

I don't like diamonds;
the emerald's "grass-lamp glow" is better;
    and unobtrusiveness is dazzling,
        upon occasion.
    Some kinds of gratitude are trying.

Poets, don't make a fuss;
the elephant's "crooked trumpet" "doth write";
    and to a tiger-book I am reading—
        I think you know the one—
    I am under obligation.

        One may be pardoned, yes I know
        one may, for love undying.

Tiger-book: Major James Corbett's *Man-Eaters of Kumaon*.

PROPRIETY

is some such word
    as the chord
        Brahms had heard
        from a bird,
sung down near the root of the throat;
it's the little downy woodpecker
        spiraling a tree—
        up up up like mercury;

    a not long
    sparrow-song
        of hayseed
        magnitude—
a tuned reticence with rigor
from strength at the source. Propriety is
        Bach's Solfegietto—
        harmonica and basso.

    The fish-spine
    on firs, on
        somber trees
        by the sea's
walls of wave-worn rock—have it; and
a moonbow and Bach's cheerful firmness
        in a minor key.
        It's an owl-and-a-pussy-

    both-content
    agreement.
        Come, come. It's
        mixed with wits;
it's not a graceful sadness. It's
resistance with bent head, like foxtail

millet's. Brahms and Bach,
no; Bach and Brahms. To thank Bach

for his song
first, is wrong.
Pardon me;
both are the
unintentional pansy-face
uncursed by self-inspection; blackened
because born that way.

ARMOR'S UNDERMINING MODESTY

At first I thought a pest
Must have alighted on my wrist.
It was a moth almost an owl,
Its wings were furred so well,
with backgammon-board wedges interlacing
on the wing—

like cloth of gold in a pattern
of scales with a hair-seal Persian
sheen. Once, self-determination
made an ax of a stone
and hacked things out with hairy paws. The consequence—

our mis-set
alphabet.

Arise, for it is day.
Even gifted scholars lose their way
through faulty etymology.
No wonder we hate poetry,
and stars and harps and the new moon. If tributes cannot
be implicit,

give me diatribes and the fragrance of iodine,
the cork oak acorn grown in Spain;
the pale-ale-eyed impersonal look
which the sales-placard gives the bock beer buck.
What is more precise than precision? Illusion.
Knights we've known,

like those familiar
now unfamiliar knights who sought the Grail, were
ducs in old Roman fashion
without the addition

of wreaths and silver rods, and armor gilded
or inlaid.

> They did not let self bar
> their usefulness to others who were
> different. Though Mars is excessive
> in being preventive,

heroes need not write an ordinall of attributes to enumerate
what they hate.

> I should, I confess,
> like to have a talk with one of them about excess,
> and armor's undermining modesty
> instead of innocent depravity.

A mirror-of-steel uninsistence should countenance
continence,

> objectified and not by chance,
> there in its frame of circumstance
> of innocence and altitude
> in an unhackneyed solitude.

There is the tarnish; and there, the imperishable wish.

II. Later Poems

LIKE A BULWARK (1956)

LIKE A BULWARK

Affirmed. Pent by power that holds it fast—
a paradox. Pent. Hard pressed,
    you take the blame and are inviolate.
        Abased at last?
        Not the tempest-tossed.
Compressed; firmed by the thrust of the blast
    till compact, like a bulwark against fate;
        lead-saluted,
        saluted by lead?
As though flying Old Glory full mast.

APPARITION OF SPLENDOR

Partaking of the miraculous
    since never known literally,
Dürer's rhinoceros
    might have startled us equally
    if black-and-white-spined elaborately.

Like another porcupine, or fern,
    the mouth in an arching egret
was too black to discern
    till exposed as a silhouette;
    but the double-embattled thistle of jet—

disadvantageous supposedly—
    has never shot a quill. Was it
some joyous fantasy,
    plain eider-eared exhibit
    of spines rooted in the sooty moss,

or "train supported by porcupines—
    a fairy's eleven yards long"? . . .
as when the lightning shines
    on thistlefine spears, among
    prongs in lanes above lanes of a shorter prong,

"with the forest for nurse," also dark
    at the base—where needle-debris
springs and shows no footmark;
    the setting for a symmetry
    you must not touch unless you are a fairy.

Maine should be pleased that its animal
    is not a waverer, and rather

than fight, lets the primed quill fall.
　　Shallow oppressor, intruder,
　　insister, you have found a resister.

THEN THE ERMINE:

"rather dead than spotted"; and believe it
    despite reason to think not,
I saw a bat by daylight;
hard to credit

but I knew that I was right. It charmed me—
    wavering like a jack-in-
the-green, weaving about me
insecurely.

Instead of hammer-handed bravado
    strategy could have chosen
momentum with a motto:
Mutare sperno

vel timere—I don't change, am not craven;
    on what ground could one
say that I am hard to frighten?
Nothing's certain.

Fail, and Lavater's physiography
    has another admirer
of skill in obscurity—
now a novelty.

So let the *palisandre* settee express it,
    "ebony violet,"
Master Corbo in full dress,
and shepherdess,

an exhilarating hoarse crow-note
    or dignity with intimacy.

Foiled explosiveness is yet
a kind of prophet,

a perfecter, and so a concealer—
        with the power of implosion;
like violets by Dürer;
even darker.

TOM FOOL AT JAMAICA

Look at Jonah embarking from Joppa, deterred by
the whale; hard going for a statesman whom nothing could
detain,
although one who would not rather die than repent.
Be infallible at your peril, for your system will fail,
and select as a model the schoolboy in Spain
who at the age of six, portrayed a mule and jockey
who had pulled up for a snail.

"There is submerged magnificence, as Victor Hugo
said." *Sentir avec ardeur*; that's it; magnetized by feeling.
Tom Fool "makes an effort and makes it oftener
than the rest"—out on April first, a day of some significance
in the ambiguous sense—the smiling
Master Atkinson's choice, with that mark of a champion, the
extra
spurt when needed. Yes, yes. "Chance

is a regrettable impurity"; like Tom Fool's
left white hind foot—an unconformity; though judging by
results, a kind of cottontail to give him confidence.
Up in the cupola comparing speeds, Fred Capossela keeps
his head.
"It's tough," he said; "but I get 'em; and why shouldn't I?
I'm relaxed, I'm confident, and I *don't bet*." Sensational. He
does not
bet on his animated

valentines—his pink and black-striped, sashed or dotted silks.
Tom Fool is "a handy horse," with a chiseled foot. You've the beat
of a dancer to a measure or harmonious rush
of a porpoise at the prow where the racers all win easily—
like centaurs' legs in tune, as when kettledrums compete;

nose rigid and suede nostrils spread, a light left hand on the
                                                    rein, till
    well—this is a rhapsody.

    Of course, speaking of champions, there was Fats Waller
with the feather touch, giraffe eyes, and that hand alighting in
    Ain't Misbehavin'! Ozzie Smith and Eubie Blake
        ennoble the atmosphere; you recall the Lippizzaner;
the time Ted Atkinson charged by on Tiger Skin—
    no pursuers in sight—cat-loping along. And you may have
                                                    seen a monkey
    on a greyhound. "But Tom Fool . . .

THE WEB ONE WEAVES OF ITALY

grows till it is not what but which,
blurred by too much. The very blasé alone could
    choose the contest or fair to which to go.
    The crossbow tournament at Gubbio?

For quiet excitement, canoe-ers
or peach fairs? or near Perugia, the mule-show;
    if not the Palio, slaying the Saracen.
    One salutes—on reviewing again

this modern *mythologica*
esopica—its nonchalances of the mind,
    that "fount by which enchanting gems are spilt."
    Are we not charmed by the result?—

quite different from what goes on
at the Sorbonne; but not entirely, since flowering
    in more than mere talent for spectacle.
    Because the heart is in it all is well.

*The greater part of stanzas 1 and 2 is quoted from an article
by Mitchell Goodman, "Festivals and Fairs for the Tourist in
Italy," New York Times, April 18, 1954.*

THE STAFF OF AESCULAPIUS

A symbol from the first, of mastery,
    experiments such as Hippocrates made
        and substituted for vague
    speculation, stayed
        the ravages of a plague.

A "going on"; yes, *anastasis* is the word
    for research a virus has defied,
        and for the virologist
    with variables still untried—
        too impassioned to desist.

Suppose that research has hit on the right one
    and a killed vaccine is effective
        say temporarily—
    for even a year—although a live
        one could give lifelong immunity,

knowledge has been gained for another attack.
    Selective injury to cancer
        cells without injury to
    normal ones—another
        gain—looks like prophecy come true.

Now, after lung resection, the surgeon fills space.
    To sponge implanted, cells following
        fluid, adhere and what
    was inert becomes living—
        that was framework. Is it not

like the master-physician's Sumerian rod?—
    staff and effigy of the animal

                which by shedding its skin
            is a sign of renewal—
                the symbol of medicine.

THE SYCAMORE

Against a gun-metal sky
I saw an albino giraffe. Without
leaves to modify,
chamois-white as
said, although partly pied near the base,
it towered where a chain of
stepping-stones lay in a stream nearby;
glamor to stir the envy

of anything in motley—
Hampshire pig, the living lucky-stone; or
all-white butterfly.
A commonplace:
there's more than just one kind of grace.
We don't like flowers that do
not wilt; they must die, and nine
she-camel-hairs aid memory.

Worthy of Imami,
the Persian—clinging to a stiffer stalk
was a little dry
thing from the grass,
in the shape of a Maltese cross,
retiringly formal
as if to say: "And there was I
like a field-mouse at Versailles."

ROSEMARY

Beauty and Beauty's son and rosemary—
Venus and Love, her son, to speak plainly—
born of the sea supposedly,
at Christmas each, in company,
braids a garland of festivity.
     Not always rosemary—

since the flight to Egypt, blooming differently.
With lancelike leaf, green but silver underneath,
its flowers—white originally—
turned blue. The herb of memory,
imitating the blue robe of Mary,
     is not too legendary

to flower both as symbol and as pungency.
Springing from stones beside the sea,
the height of Christ when thirty-three—
it feeds on dew and to the bee
"hath a dumb language"; is in reality
     a kind of Christmas-tree.

STYLE

revives in Escudero's constant of the plumbline
axis of the hairfine moon—his counter-camber of the skater.
No more fanatical adjuster
    of the tilted hat
than Escudero; of tempos others can't combine.
    And we—besides evolving
    the classic silhouette, Dick Button whittled slender—

have an Iberian-American champion yet,
the deadly Etchebaster. Entranced, were you not, by Soledad?
black-clad solitude that is not sad;
    like a letter from
Casals; or perhaps say literal alphabet-
    S soundholes in a 'cello
    set contradictorily; or should we call her

la lagarta? or bamboos with fireflies a-glitter;
or glassy lake and the whorls which a vertical stroke brought
             about,
of the paddle half-turned coming out.
    As if bisecting
a viper, she can dart down three times and recover
    without a disaster, having
    been a bull-fighter. Well; she has a forgiver.

Etchebaster's art, his catlike ease, his mousing pose,
his genius for anticipatory tactics, preclude envy
as the traditional unwavy
    Sandeman sailor
    Is Escudero's; the guitar, Rosario's—

wrist-rest for a dangling hand
that's suddenly set humming fast fast fast and faster.

There is no suitable simile. It is as though
the equidistant three tiny arcs of seeds in a banana
had been conjoined by Palestrina;
it is like the eyes,
or say the face, of Palestrina by El Greco.
O Escudero, Soledad,
Rosario Escudero, Etchebaster!

LOGIC AND "THE MAGIC FLUTE"

Up winding stair,
here, where, in what theater lost?
was I seeing a ghost—
a reminder at least
        of a sunbeam or moonbeam
that has not a waist?
        By hasty hop
        or accomplished mishap,
the magic flute and harp
somehow confused themselves
        with China's precious wentletrap.

Near Life and Time
in their peculiar catacomb,
abalonean gloom
and an intrusive hum
        pervaded the mammoth cast's
small audience-room.
        Then out of doors,
        where interlacing pairs
of skaters raced from rink
to ramp, a demon roared
        as if down flights of marble stairs:

" 'What is love and
shall I ever have it?' " The truth
is simple. Banish sloth,
fetter-feigning uncouth
        fraud. Trapper Love with noble
noise, the magic sleuth,
        as bird-notes prove—

first telecolor-trove—
illogically wove
what logic can't unweave:
one need not shoulder, need not shove.

BLESSED IS THE MAN

who does not sit in the seat of the scoffer—
   the man who does not denigrate, depreciate, denunciate;
      who is not "characteristically intemperate,"
who does not "excuse, retreat, equivocate; and will be heard."

(Ah, Giorgione! there are those who mongrelize
   and those who heighten anything they touch; although it
                                             may well be
      that if Giorgione's self-portrait were not said to be he,
it might not take my fancy. Blessed the geniuses who know

that egomania is not a duty.)
   "Diversity, controversy; tolerance"—in that "citadel
      of learning" we have a fort that ought to armor us well.
Blessed is the man who "takes the risk of a decision"—asks

himself the question: "Would it solve the problem?
   Is it right as I see it? Is it in the best interests of all?"
      Alas. Ulysses' companions are now political—
living self-indulgently until the moral sense is drowned,

having lost all power of comparison,
   thinking license emancipates one, "slaves whom they
                                          themselves have bound."
      Brazen authors, downright soiled and downright spoiled, as
                                             if sound
and exceptional, are the old quasi-modish counterfeit,

mitin-proofing conscience against character.
   Affronted by "private lies and public shame," blessed is the
                                                author
      who favors what the supercilious do *not* favor—
who will not comply. Blessed, the unaccommodating man.

Blessed the man whose faith is different
        from possessiveness—of a kind not framed by "things which
                        do appear"—
    who will not visualize defeat, too intent to cower;
whose illumined eye has seen the shaft that gilds the sultan's
                        tower.

O TO BE A DRAGON (1959)

O TO BE A DRAGON

If I, like Solomon, . . .
could have my wish—

my wish . . . O to be a dragon,
a symbol of the power of Heaven—of silkworm
size or immense; at times invisible.
Felicitous phenomenon!

I MAY, I MIGHT, I MUST

If you will tell me why the fen
appears impassable, I then
will tell you why I think that I
can get across it if I try.

TO A CHAMELEON

Hid by the august foliage and fruit of the grape-vine
  twine
    your anatomy
      round the pruned and polished stem,
        Chameleon.
        Fire laid upon
      an emerald as long as
    the Dark King's massy
  one,
could not snap the spectrum up for food as you have done.

A JELLY-FISH

Visible, invisible,
  a fluctuating charm
an amber-tinctured amethyst
  inhabits it, your arm
approaches and it opens
  and it closes; you had meant
to catch it and it quivers;
  you abandon your intent.

VALUES IN USE

I attended school and I liked the place—
grass and little locust-leaf shadows like lace.

Writing was discussed. They said, "We create
values in the process of living, daren't await

their historic progress." Be abstract
and you'll wish you'd been specific; it's a fact.

What was I studying? Values in use,
"judged on their own ground." Am I still abstruse?

Walking along, a student said offhand,
" 'Relevant' and 'plausible' were words I understand."

A pleasing statement, anonymous friend.
Certainly the means must not defeat the end.

HOMETOWN PIECE FOR
MESSRS. ALSTON AND REESE

To the tune:
"Li'l baby, don't say a word: Mama goin' to buy you a
                                                    mocking-bird.
Bird don't sing: Mama goin' to sell it and buy a brass ring."

"Millennium," yes; "pandemonium"!
Roy Campanella leaps high. Dodgerdom

crowned, had Johnny Podres on the mound.
Buzzie Bavasi and the Press gave ground;

the team slapped, mauled, and asked the Yankees' match,
"How did you feel when Sandy Amoros made the catch?"

"I said to myself"—pitcher for all innings—
"as I walked back to the mound I said, 'Everything's

getting better and better.'" (Zest: they've zest.
"'Hope springs eternal in the Brooklyn breast.'"

And would the Dodger Band in 8, row 1, relax
if they saw the collector of income tax?

Ready with a tune if that should occur:
"Why Not Take All of Me—All of Me, Sir?")

Another series. Round-tripper Duke at bat,
"Four hundred feet from home-plate"; more like that.

A neat bunt, please; a cloud-breaker, a drive
like Jim Gilliam's great big one. Hope's alive.

Homered, flied out, fouled? Our "stylish stout"
so nimble Campanella will have him out.

A-squat in double-headers four hundred times a day,
he says that in a measure the pleasure is the pay:

catcher to pitcher, a nice easy throw
almost as if he'd just told it to go.

Willie Mays should be a Dodger. He should—
a lad for Roger Craig and Clem Labine to elude;

but you have an omen, pennant-winning Peewee,
on which we are looking superstitiously.

Ralph Branca has Preacher Roe's number; recall?
and there's Don Bessent; he can really fire the ball.

As for Gil Hodges, in custody of first—
"He'll do it by himself." Now a specialist—versed

in an extension reach far into the box seats—
he lengthens up, leans and gloves the ball. He defeats

expectation by a whisker. The modest star,
irked by one misplay, is no hero by a hair;

in a strikeout slaughter when what could matter more,
he lines a homer to the signboard and has changed the score.

Then for his nineteenth season, a home run—
with four of six runs batted in—Carl Furillo's the big gun;

almost dehorned the foe—has fans dancing in delight.
Jake Pitler and his Playground "get a Night"—

Jake, that hearty man, made heartier by a harrier
who can bat as well as field—Don Demeter.

Shutting them out for nine innings—hitter too—
Carl Erskine leaves Cimoli nothing to do.

Take off the goat-horns, Dodgers, that egret
which two very fine base-stealers can offset.

You've got plenty: Jackie Robinson
and Campy and big Newk, and Dodgerdom again
watching everything you do. You won last year. Come on.

ENOUGH

Jamestown, 1607–1957

Some in the Godspeed, the Susan C.,
others in the Discovery,

found their too earthly paradise,
a paradise in which hope dies,

found pests and pestilence instead,
the living outnumbered by the dead.

The same reward for best and worst
doomed communism, tried at first.

Three acres each, initiative,
six bushels paid back, they could live

Captain Dale became kidnaper—
the master—lawless when the spur

was desperation, even though
his victim had let her victim go—

Captain John Smith. Poor Powhatan
was forced to make peace, embittered man.

Then teaching—insidious recourse—
enhancing Pocahontas, flowered of course

in marriage. John Rolfe fell in love
with her and she—in rank above

what she became—renounced her name
yet found her status not too tame.

The crested moss-rose casts a spell;
and bud of solid green as well;

old deep pink one with fragrant wings
imparting balsam scent that clings

where redbrown tanbark holds the sun—
path enticing beyond comparison.

Not to begin with. No select
artlessly perfect French effect

mattered at first. (Don't speak in rhyme
of maddened men in starving-time.)

Tested until so unnatural
that one became a cannibal.

Marriage, tobacco, and slavery,
initiated liberty

when the Deliverance brought seed
of that now controversial weed—

a blameless plant-Red-Ridinghood.
Blameless, but who knows what is good?

The victims of a search for gold
cast yellow soil into the hold.

With nothing but the feeble tower
to mark the site that did not flower,

could the most ardent have been sure
that they had done what would endure?

It was enough; it is enough
if present faith mend partial proof.

MELCHIOR VULPIUS

c. 1560–1615

a contrapuntalist—
> composer of chorales
and wedding-hymns to Latin words
but best of all an anthem:
> "God be praised for conquering faith
> which feareth neither pain nor death."

We have to trust this art—
> this mastery which none
can understand. Yet someone has
acquired it and is able to
> direct it. Mouse-skin-bellows'-breath
> expanding into rapture saith

"Hallelujah." Almost
> utmost absolutist
and fugue-ist, Amen; slowly building
from miniature thunder,
> crescendos antidoting death—
> love's signature cementing faith.

NO BETTER THAN
A "WITHERED DAFFODIL"

Ben Jonson said he was? "O I could still
like melting snow upon some craggy hill,
    drop, drop, drop, drop."

I too until I saw that French brocade
blaze green as though some lizard in the shade
    became exact—

set off by replicas of violet—
like Sidney, leaning in his striped jacket
    against a lime—

a work of art. And I too seemed to be
an insouciant rester by a tree—
    no daffodil.

IN THE PUBLIC GARDEN

Boston has a festival—
compositely for all—
and nearby, cupolas of learning
(crimson, blue, and gold) that
    have made education individual.

My first—an exceptional,
    an almost scriptural—
taxi-driver to Cambridge from Back Bay
said, as we went along, "They
    make some fine young men at Harvard." I recall

the summer when Faneuil Hall
    had its weathervane with gold ball
and grasshopper, gilded again by
a -leafer and -jack
    till it glittered. Spring can be a miracle

there—a more than usual
    bouquet of what is vernal—
"pear blossoms whiter than the clouds," pin-
oak leaves that barely show
    when other trees are making shade, besides small

fairy iris suitable
    for Dulcinea del
Toboso; O yes, and snowdrops
in the snow, that smell like
    violets. Despite secular bustle,

let me enter King's Chapel
    to hear them sing: "My work be praise while
others go and come. No more a stranger

or a guest but like a child
    at home." A chapel or a festival

    means giving what is mutual,
    even if irrational:
black sturgeon-eggs—a camel
from Hamadan, Iran;
    a jewel, or, what is more unusual,

    silence—after a word-waterfall of the banal—
    as unattainable
as freedom. And what is freedom for?
For "self-discipline," as our
    hardest-working citizen has said—a school;

    it is for "freedom to toil"
    with a feel for the tool.
Those in the trans-shipment camp must have
a skill. With hope of freedom hanging
    by a thread—some gather medicinal

    herbs which they can sell.
    Ineligible if they ail.
                Well?

There are those who will talk for an hour
without telling you why they have
    come. And I? This is no madrigal—
    no medieval gradual.
    It is a grateful tale—
without that radiance which poets
are supposed to have—
    unofficial, unprofessional. But still one need not fail

    to wish poetry well
    where intellect is habitual—

glad that the Muses have a home and swans—
that legend can be factual;
   happy that Art, admired in general,
   is always actually personal.

THE ARCTIC OX (OR GOAT)

*Derived from "Golden Fleece of the Arctic," by John J. Teal,
Jr., who rears musk oxen on his farm in Vermont, as set forth
by him in the March 1958 issue of the* Atlantic Monthly.

To wear the arctic fox
you have to kill it. Wear
   qiviut—the underwool of the arctic ox—
pulled off it like a sweater;
your coat is warm; your conscience, better.

I would like a suit of
qiviut, so light I did not
   know I had it on; and in the
course of time, another
since I had not had to murder

the "goat" that grew the fleece
that made the first. The musk ox
   has no musk and it is not an ox—
illiterate epithet.
Bury your nose in one when wet.

It smells of water, nothing else,
and browses goatlike on
   hind legs. Its great distinction
is not egocentric scent
but that it is intelligent.

Chinchillas, otters, water-rats,
and beavers, keep us warm
   but think! a "musk ox" grows six pounds

of *qiviut*; the cashmere ram,
three ounces—that is all—of pashm.

Lying in an exposed spot,
basking in the blizzard,
   these ponderosos could dominate
the rare-hairs market in Kashan and yet
you could not have a choicer pet.

They join you as you work;
love jumping in and out of holes,
   play in water with the children,
learn fast, know their names,
will open gates and invent games.

While not incapable
of courtship, they may find its
   servitude and flutter, too much
like Procrustes' bed;
so some decide to stay unwed.

Camels are snobbish
and sheep, unintelligent;
   water buffaloes, neurasthenic—
even murderous.
Reindeer seem over-serious,

whereas these scarce *qivies*,
with golden fleece and winning ways,
   outstripping every fur-bearer—
there in Vermont quiet—
could demand Bold Ruler's diet:

Mountain Valley water,
dandelions, carrots, oats—

encouraged as well by bed
made fresh three times a day—
to roll and revel in the hay.

Insatiable for willow
leaves alone, our goatlike
   qivi-curvi-capricornus
sheds down ideal for a nest.
Song-birds find *qiviut* best.

Suppose you had a bag
of it; you could spin a pound
   into a twenty-four-or-five-
mile thread—one, forty-ply—
that will not shrink in any dye.

If you fear that you are
reading an advertisement,
   you are. If we can't be cordial
to these creatures' fleece,
I think that we deserve to freeze.

SAINT NICHOLAS,

might I, if you can find it, be given
a chameleon with tail
that curls like a watch spring; and vertical
on the body—including the face—pale
  tiger-stripes, about seven;
      (the melanin in the skin
        having been shaded from the sun by thin
          bars; the spinal dome
              beaded along the ridge
              as if it were platinum)?

If you can find no striped chameleon,
might I have a dress or suit—
I guess you have heard of it—of *qiviut*?
and to wear with it, a taslon shirt, the drip-dry fruit
  of research second to none;
      sewn, I hope, by Excello;
        as for buttons to keep down the collar-points, no.
          The shirt could be white—
              and be "worn before six,"
              either in daylight or at night.

But don't give me, if I can't have the dress,
a trip to Greenland, or grim
trip to the moon. The moon should come here. Let him
make the trip down, spread on my dark floor some dim
  marvel, and if a success
      that I stoop to pick up and wear,
        I could ask nothing more. A thing yet more rare,
          though, and different,
              would be this: Hans von Marées'
              St. Hubert, kneeling with head bent,

erect—in velvet and tense with restraint—
hand hanging down: the horse, free.
Not the original, of course. Give me
a postcard of the scene—huntsman and divinity—
   hunt-mad Hubert startled into a saint
     by a stag with a Figure entined.
      But why tell you what you must have divined?
      Saint Nicholas, O Santa Claus,
        would it not be the most
        prized gift that ever was!

FOR FEBRUARY 14TH

Saint Valentine,
although late, would "some interested law
impelled to plod in the poem's cause"
be permitted a line?

Might you have liked a stone
from a De Beers Consolidated Mine?
or badger-neat saber-thronged thistle
of Palestine—the leaves alone

down'd underneath,
worth a touch? or that mimosa-leafed vine
called an "alexander's armillary
sphere" fanning out in a wreath?

Or did the ark
preserve paradise-birds with jet-black plumes,
whose descendants might serve as presents?
But questioning is the mark

of a pest! Why think
only of animals in connection
with the ark or the wine Noah drank?
but that the ark did not sink.

COMBAT CULTURAL

One likes to see a laggard rook's high
speed at sunset to outfly the dark,
        or a mount well schooled for a medal;
tucked up front legs for the barrier—
        or team of leapers turned aerial.

I recall a documentary
of Cossacks: a visual fugue, a mist
        of swords that seemed to sever
heads from bodies—feet stepping as though through
        harp-strings in a scherzo. However,

the quadrille of Old Russia for me:
with aimlessly drooping handkerchief
        snapped like the crack of a whip;
a deliriously spun-out-level
        frock-coat skirt, unswirled and a-droop

in remote promenade. Let me see . . .
Old Russia, I said? Cold Russia
        this time: the prize bunnyhug
platform-piece of experts in the
        trip-and-slug of wrestlers in a rug.

"Sacked" and ready for bed apparently—
with a jab, a kick, pinned to the wall,
        they work toward the edge and stick;
stagger off, and one is victim of a
        flipflop—leg having circled leg as thick.

"Some art, because of high quality,
is unlikely to command high sales";
        yes, yes; but here, oh no;

not with the frozen North's Nan-ai-ans
    of the sack in their tight touch-and-go.

  These battlers, dressed identically—
just one person—may, by seeming twins,
    point a moral, should I confess;
we must cement the parts of any
    objective symbolic of *sagesse*.

LEONARDO DA VINCI'S

Saint Jerome and his lion
in that hermitage
of walls half gone,
share sanctuary for a sage—
joint-frame for impassioned ingenious
Jerome versed in language—
and for a lion like one on the skin of which
Hercules' club made no impression.

The beast, received as a guest,
although some monks fled—
with its paw dressed
that a desert thorn had made red—
stayed as guard of the monastery ass . . .
which vanished, having fed
its guard, Jerome assumed. The guest then, like an ass,
was made to carry wood and did not resist,

but before long, recognized
the ass and consigned
its terrorized
thieves' whole camel-train to chagrined
Saint Jerome. The vindicated beast and
saint somehow became twinned;
and now, since they behaved and also looked alike,
their lionship seems officialized.

Pacific yet passionate—
for if not both, how
could he be great?
Jerome—reduced by what he'd been through—
with tapering waist no matter what he ate,
left us the Vulgate. That in *Leo*,

the Nile's rise grew food checking famine,
    made lion's-mouth fountains appropriate,

        if not universally,
            at least not obscure.
        And here, though hardly a summary, astronomy
            or pale paint makes the golden pair
in Leonardo da Vinci's sketch—seem
            sun-dyed. Blaze on, picture,
saint, beast; and Lion Haile Selassie, with household
            lions as symbol of sovereignty.

TELL ME, TELL ME (1966)

GRANITE AND STEEL

Enfranchising cable, silvered by the sea,
   of woven wire, grayed by the mist,
   and Liberty dominate the Bay—
   her feet as one on shattered chains,
   once whole links wrought by Tyranny.

Caged Circe of steel and stone,
   her parent German ingenuity.
"O catenary curve" from tower to pier,
implacable enemy of the mind's deformity,
of man's uncompunctious greed
his crass love of crass priority
    just recently
obstructing acquiescent feet
about to step ashore when darkness fell
   without a cause,
as if probity had not joined our cities
   in the sea.

"O path amid the stars
crossed by the seagull's wing!"
"O radiance that doth inherit me!"
—affirming inter-acting harmony!

Untried expedient, untried; then tried;
way out; way in; romantic passageway
first seen by the eye of the mind,
then by the eye. O steel! O stone!
Climactic ornament, a double rainbow,
as if inverted by French perspicacity,
   John Roebling's monument,
   German tenacity's also;
   composite span—an actuality.

IN LIEU OF THE LYRE

One debarred from enrollment at Harvard,
may have seen towers and been shown the Yard—
animated by Madame de Boufflers' choice rhymes:
Sentir avec ardeur: with fire; yes, with passion;
rime-prose revived also by word-wizard Achilles—
        Dr. Fang.

The *Harvard Advocate*'s select formal-informal
invitation to Harvard made grateful, Brooklyn's (or Mexico's)
        ineditos—
one whose "French aspect" was invented by
        Professor Levin,
a too outspoken outraged refugee from clichés particularly,
        who was proffered redress
        by the Lowell House Press—
Vermont Stinehour Press, rather. (No careless statements
to Kirkland House; least of all inexactness in quoting a fact.)

        To the *Advocate, gratia sum*
        unavoidably lame as I am, verbal pilgrim
like Thomas Bewick, drinking from his hat-brim,
drops spilled from a waterfall, denominated later by him
        a crystalline Fons Bandusian miracle.

It occurs to the guest—if someone had confessed it in time—
that you might have preferred to the waterfall, pilgrim and
                        hat-brim,
        a valuable axiom such as
"a force at rest is at rest because balanced by some other force,"
or "catenary and triangle together hold the span in place"
        (of a bridge),

or a too often forgotten surely relevant thing, that Roebling cable
was invented by John A. Roebling.

These reflections, Mr. Davis,
in lieu of the lyre.

THE MIND, INTRACTABLE THING

even with its own ax to grind, sometimes
   helps others. Why can't it help me?

      O imagnifico,
wizard in words—poet, was it, as
Alfredo Panzini defined you?
Weren't you refracting just now
on my eye's half-closed triptych
   the image, enhanced, of a glen—
"the foxgrape festoon as sere leaves fell"
on the sand-pale dark byroad, one leaf adrift
   from the thin-twigged persimmon; again,

      a bird—Arizona
caught-up-with, uncatchable cuckoo
after two hours' pursuit, zigzagging
road-runner, stenciled in black
stripes all over, the tail
   windmilling up to defy me?
You understand terror, know how to deal
with pent-up emotion, a ballad, witchcraft.
   I don't. O Zeus and O Destiny!

Unafraid of what's done,
undeterred by apparent defeat,
you, imagnifico, unafraid
of disparagers, death, dejection,
have out-wiled the Mermaid of Zennor,
   made wordcraft irresistible:
reef, wreck, lost lad, and "sea-foundered bell"—
as near a thing as we have to a king—
   craft with which I don't know how to deal.

DREAM

*After coming on Jerome S. Shipman's comment concerning
academic appointments for artists.*

The committee—now a permanent body—
      formed to do but one thing,
discover positions for artists, was worried, then happy;
rejoiced to have magnetized Bach and his family
  "to Northwestern," besides five harpsichords
        without which he would not leave home.
For his methodic unmetronomic melodic diversity
contrapuntally appointedly persistently
      irresistibly Fate-like Bach—find me words.

Expected to create for university
        occasions, inventions with wing,
was no trouble after master-classes (stiffer in Germany),

each week a cantata; chorales, fugues, concerti!
  Here, students craved a teacher and each student worked.
      Jubilation! Re-rejoicings! Felicity!
      Repeated fugue-like, all of it, to infinity.
  (Note too that over-worked Bach was not irked.)

Haydn, when he had heard of Bach's billowing sail,
begged Prince Esterházy to lend him to Yale.
Master-mode expert fugue-al forms since, prevail.

      Dazzling nonsense . . . I imagine it? Ah! nach
      enough. J. Sebastian—born at Eisenach:
      its coat-of-arms in my dream: BACH PLAYS BACH!

OLD AMUSEMENT PARK

Before it became LaGuardia Airport.

Hurry, worry, unwary
visitor, never vary
   the pressure till nearly bat-blind.
     A predicament so dire could not
     occur in this rare spot—

where crowds flock to the tramcar
rattling greenish caterpillar,
   as bowling-ball thunder
     quivers the air. The park's elephant
     slowly lies down aslant;

a pygmy replica then rides
the mound the back provides.
   Jet black, a furry pony sits
     down like a dog, has an innocent air—
     no tricks—the best act there.

It's all like the never-ending
Ferris-wheel ascending
   picket-fenced pony-rides (ten cents).
     A businessman, the pony-paddock boy
     locks his equestrian toy—

flags flying, fares collected,
shooting gallery neglected—
   half-official, half-sequestered,
     limber-slouched against a post,
     and tells a friend what matters least.

It's the old park in a nutshell,
like its tame-wild carrousel—

the exhilarating peak
when the triumph is reflective
and confusion, retroactive.

AN EXPEDIENT—LEONARDO DA VINCI'S—
AND A QUERY

It was patience
   protecting the soul as clothing the body
from cold, so that "great wrongs
     were powerless to vex"—
     and problems that seemed to perplex
   him bore fruit, memory
making past present—
like "the grasp of the gourd,
       sure and firm."

"None too dull to
   be able to do one thing well. Unworthy
of praise, an orator
     who knows only one word,
     lacking variety." Height deterred
   from his verdure, any
polecat or snake that
might have burdened his vine:
       it kept them away.

With a passion,
   he drew flowers, acorns, rocks—intensively,
like Giotto, made Nature
     the test, imitation—
     Rome's taint—did not taint what he'd done.
   He saw as treachery
the all-in-one-mold.
Peerless, venerated
     by all, he succumbed

to dejection. Could not
   the Leda with face matchless minutely—

have lightened the blow?
    "Sad" . . . Could not Leonardo
have said, "I agree; proof refutes me.
If all is mobility,
    mathematics won't do":
instead of, "Tell me if anything
    at all has been done?"

W. S. LANDOR

There
is someone I can bear—
    "a master of indignation . . .
meant for a soldier
    converted to letters," who could

throw
a man through the window,
    yet, "tender toward plants," say, "Good God,
the violets!" (below).
    "Accomplished in every

style
and tint"—considering meanwhile
    infinity and eternity,
he could only say, "I'll
    talk about them when I understand them."

TO A GIRAFFE

If it is unpermissible, in fact fatal
to be personal and undesirable

to be literal—detrimental as well
if the eye is not innocent—does it mean that

one can live only on top leaves that are small
reachable only by a beast that is tall?—

of which the giraffe is the best example—
the unconversational animal.

When plagued by the psychological,
a creature can be unbearable

that could have been irresistible;
or to be exact, exceptional

since less conversational
than some emotionally-tied-in-knots animal.

    After all
consolations of the metaphysical
can be profound. In Homer, existence

is flawed; transcendence, conditional;
"the journey from sin to redemption, perpetual."

CHARITY OVERCOMING ENVY

*Late-fifteenth-century tapestry, Flemish or French, in the
Burrell Collection, Glasgow Art Gallery and Museum.*

Have you time for a story
   (depicted in tapestry)?
Charity, riding an elephant,
on a "mosaic of flowers," faces Envy,
the flowers "bunched together, not rooted."
Envy, on a dog, is worn down by obsession,
his greed (since of things owned by others
he can only take *some*). Crouching uneasily
in the flowered filigree, among wide weeds
   indented by scallops that swirl,
little flattened-out sunflowers,
thin arched coral stems, and—ribbed horizontally—
slivers of green, Envy, on his dog,
   looks up at the elephant,
cowering away from her, his cheek scarcely scratched.
   He is saying, "O Charity, pity me, Deity!
   O pitiless Destiny,
   what will become of me,
maimed by Charity—*Caritas*—sword unsheathed
over me yet? Blood stains my cheek. I am hurt."
In chest armor over chain mail, a steel shirt
to the knee, he repeats, "I am hurt."
The elephant, at no time borne down by self-pity,
   convinces the victim
that Destiny is not devising a plot.

The problem is mastered—insupportably
tiring when it was impending.

Deliverance accounts for what sounds like an axiom.

The Gordian knot need not be cut.

BLUE BUG

Upon seeing Dr. Raworth Williams' Blue Bug with seven other ponies, photographed by Thomas McAvoy: Sports Illustrated.

In this camera shot,
from that fine print in which you hide
(eight-pony portrait from the side),
    you seem to recognize
    a recognizing eye,
        limber Bug.
Only partly said, perhaps, it has been implied
that you seem to be the one to ride.

I don't know how you got your name
    and don't like to inquire.
        Nothing more punitive than the pest
    who says, "I'm trespassing," and
does it just the same.
    I've guessed, I think.
        I like a face that seems a nest,

a "mere container for the eye"—
    triangle-cornered—and
        pitchfork-pronged ears stiffly parallel:
    bug brother to an Arthur
Mitchell dragonfly,
    speeding to left,
        speeding to right; reversible,

like "turns in an ancient Chinese
    melody, a thirteen
            twisted silk-string three-finger solo."
        There they are, Yellow River-
scroll accuracies

of your version
of something similar—polo.

Restating it:
pelo, I turn,
on *polos*, a pivot.

If a little elaborate,
Redon (Odilon) brought it to mind,
his thought of the eye,
of revolving—combined somehow with pastime—
pastime that is work,
muscular docility,
also mentality,

as in the acrobat Li Siau Than,
gibbon-like but limberer,
defying gravity,
nether side arched up,
cup on head not upset—
China's very most ingenious man.

ARTHUR MITCHELL

Slim dragonfly
too rapid for the eye
   to cage—
contagious gem of virtuosity—
make visible, mentality.
Your jewels of mobility

    reveal
       and veil
          a peacock-tail.

BASEBALL AND WRITING

Suggested by post-game broadcasts.

Fanaticism? No. Writing is exciting
and baseball is like writing.
   You can never tell with either
     how it will go
     or what you will do;
   generating excitement—
   a fever in the victim—
   pitcher, catcher, fielder, batter.
        Victim in what category?
*Owl*man watching from the press box?
        To whom does it apply?
        Who is excited? Might it be I?

It's a pitcher's battle all the way—a duel—
a catcher's, as, with cruel
   puma paw, Elston Howard lumbers lightly
     back to plate. (His spring
     de-winged a bat swing.)
   They have that killer instinct;
   yet Elston—whose catching
   arm has hurt them all with the bat—
        when questioned, says, unenviously,
"I'm very satisfied. We won."
        Shorn of the batting crown, says, "We";
        robbed by a technicality.

When three players on a side play three positions
and modify conditions,
   the massive run need not be everything.
     "Going, going . . ." Is
     it? Roger Maris

has it, running fast. You will
never see a finer catch. Well . . .
  "Mickey, leaping like the devil"—why
              gild it, although deer sounds better—
snares what was speeding towards its treetop nest,
              one-handing the souvenir-to-be
              meant to be caught by you or me.

Assign Yogi Berra to Cape Canaveral;
he could handle any missile.
  He is no feather. "Strike! . . . Strike *two!*"
      Fouled back. A blur.
      It's gone. You would infer
    that the bat had eyes.
    He put the wood to that one.
Praised, Skowron says, "Thanks, Mel.
  I think I helped a *little* bit."
              All business, each, and modesty.
        Blanchard, Richardson, Kubek, Boyer.
              In that galaxy of nine, say which
              won the pennant? *Each*. It was he.

Those two magnificent saves from the knee—throws
by Boyer, finesses in twos—
    like Whitey's three kinds of pitch and pre-
              diagnosis
      with pick-off psychosis.
    Pitching is a large subject.
  Your arm, too true at first, can learn to
catch the corners—even trouble
              Mickey Mantle. ("Grazed a Yankee!
My baby pitcher, Montejo!"
              With some pedagogy,
              you'll be tough, premature prodigy.)

They crowd him and curve him and aim for the knees. Trying
indeed! The secret implying:
    "I can stand here, bat held steady."
      One may suit him;
      none has hit him.
    Imponderables smite him.
    Muscle kinks, infections, spike wounds
    require food, rest, respite from ruffians. (Drat it!
        Celebrity costs privacy!)
Cow's milk, "tiger's milk," soy milk, carrot juice,
        brewer's yeast (high-potency)—
        concentrates presage victory

sped by Luis Arroyo, Hector Lopez—
deadly in a pinch. And "Yes,
    it's work; I want you to bear down,
      but enjoy it
      while you're doing it."
    Mr. Houk and Mr. Sain,
    if you have a rummage sale,
    don't sell Roland Sheldon or Tom Tresh.
        Studded with stars in belt and crown,
the Stadium is an adastrium.
        O flashing Orion,
        your stars are muscled like the lion.

TO VICTOR HUGO OF MY CROW PLUTO

"Even when the bird is walking we know that it has wings."
                                        —VICTOR HUGO

        Of:
            my crow
            Pluto,

            the true
            Plato,

            azzurro-
            negro

            green-blue
            rainbow—

            Victor Hugo,
            it is true

            we know
            that the crow

            "has wings," how-
            ever pigeon-toe-

            inturned on grass. We do.
                (adagio)

            Vivo-
            rosso

            "corvo,"
            although

con dizio-
nario

io parlo
Italiano—

this pseudo
Esperanto

which, savio
ucello

you speak too—
my vow and motto

(botto e totto)
io giuro

è questo
credo:

lucro
è peso morto.

And so
dear crow—

gioièllo
mio—

I have to
let you go;

a bel bosco
generoso,

tuttuto
vagabondo,

serafino
uvaceo

Sunto,
oltremarino

verecondo
Plato, addio.

Impromptu equivalents for *esperanto madinusa* (made in U.S.A.) for those who might not resent them.

azzurro-negro: blue-black
vivorosso: lively
con dizionario: with dictionary
savio ucello: knowing bird
botto e totto: vow and motto
io giuro: I swear
è questo credo: is this credo
lucro è peso morto: profit is a
   dead weight

gioièllo mio: my jewel
a bel bosco: to lovely woods
tuttuto vagabondo: complete
   gypsy
serafino uvaceo: grape-black
   seraph
sunto: in short
verecondo: modest

RESCUE WITH YUL BRYNNER

Appointed special consultant to the United Nations High Commissioner for Refugees, 1959–1960.

"Recital? 'Concert' is the word,"
and stunning, by the Budapest Symphony—
    displaced but not deterred—
listened to by me,
        though with detachment then,
            like a grasshopper that did not
            know it missed the mower, a pygmy citizen;
                a case, I'd say, of too slow a grower.
There were thirty million; there are thirteen still—
healthy to begin with, kept waiting till they're ill.
History judges. It will
salute Winnipeg's incredible
conditions: "Ill; no sponsor; and no kind of skill."
        Odd—a reporter with guitar—a puzzle.
        Mysterious Yul did not come to dazzle.

Magic bird with multiple tongue—
five tongues—equipped for a crazy twelve-month tramp
    (a plod), he flew among
the damned, found each camp
        where hope had slowly died
            (some had never seen a plane).
            Instead of feathering himself, he exemplified
                the rule that, self-applied, omits the gold.
He said, "You may feel strange; nothing matters less.
Nobody notices; you'll find some happiness.
No new 'big fear'; no distress."
Yul can sing—twin of an enchantress—

elephant-borne dancer in silver-spangled dress,
  swirled aloft by trunk, with star-tipped wand, Tamara,
  as true to the beat as *Symphonia Hungarica*.

Head bent down over the guitar,
he barely seemed to hum; ended "all come home";
  did not smile; came by air;
did not have to come.
    The guitar's an event.
      Guests of honor can't dance; don't smile.
      "Have a home?" a boy asks. "Shall we live in a tent?"
      "In a house," Yul answers. His neat cloth hat
has nothing like the glitter reflected on the face
of milkweed-witch seed-brown dominating a palace
that was nothing like the place
where he is now. His deliberate pace
is a king's, however. "You'll have plenty of space."
  Yule—Yul log for the Christmas-fire tale-spinner—
  of fairy tales that can come true: Yul Brynner.

CARNEGIE HALL: RESCUED

"It spreads," the campaign—carried on
by long-distance telephone,
    with "Saint Diogenes
        supreme commander."
    At the fifty-ninth minute
        of the eleventh hour, a rescuer

makes room for Mr. Carnegie's
music hall, which by degrees
    became (becomes)
        our music stronghold
    (accented on the "né," as
        perhaps you don't have to be told).

Paderewski's "palladian
majesty" made it a fane;
    Tschaikovsky, of course,
        on the opening
    night, 1891;
        and Gilels, a master, playing.

With Andrew C. and Mr. R.,
"our spearhead, Mr. Star"—
    in music, Stern—
        has grown forensic,
    and by civic piety
        has saved our city panic;

rescuer of a music hall
menaced by the "cannibal
    of real estate"—bulldozing potentate,

land-grabber, the human crab
left cowering like a neonate.

As Venice "in defense of children"
has forbidden for the citizen,
by "a tradition of
noble behavior,
dress too strangely shaped or scant,"
posterity may impute error

to our demolishers of glory. Jean Cocteau's "Preface
to the Past" contains the phrase
"When very young my dream
was of pure glory."
Must he say "was" of his "light
dream," which confirms our glittering story?

They need their old brown home. Cellist,
violinist, pianist—
used to unmusical
impenetralia's
massive masonry—have found
reasons to return. Fantasias

of praise and rushings to the front
dog the performer. We hunt
you down, Saint Diogenes—
are thanking you for glittering,
for rushing to the rescue
as if you'd heard yourself performing.

TELL ME, TELL ME

        where might there be a refuge for me
         from egocentricity
and its propensity to bisect,
mis-state, misunderstand
      and obliterate continuity?
          Why, oh why, one ventures to ask, set
flatness on some cindery pinnacle
as if on Lord Nelson's revolving diamond rosette?

      It appeared: gem, burnished rarity
        and peak of delicacy—
in contrast with grievance touched off on
any ground—the absorbing
        geometry of a fantasy:
          a James, Miss Potter, Chinese
"passion for the particular," of a
tired man who yet, at dusk,
        cut a masterpiece of cerise—

      for no tailor-and-cutter jury—
        only a few mice to see,
who "breathed inconsistency and drank
contradiction," dazzled
      not by the sun but by "shadowy
        possibility." (I'm referring
to Henry James and Beatrix Potter's Tailor.)
I vow, rescued tailor
        of Gloucester, I am going

      to flee; by engineering strategy—
        the viper's traffic-knot—flee
to metaphysical newmown hay,
honeysuckle, or woods fragrance.

Might one say or imply T.S.V.P.—
    Taisez-vous? "Please" does not make sense
to a refugee from verbal ferocity; I am
perplexed. Even so, "deference";
      yes, deference may be my defense.

A *précis?*
    In this told-backward biography
    of how the cat's mice when set free
by the tailor of Gloucester, finished
the Lord Mayor's cerise coat—
    the tailor's tale ended captivity
      in two senses. Besides having told
of a coat which made the tailor's fortune,
it rescued a reader
      from being driven mad by a scold.

SAINT VALENTINE,

permitted to assist you, let me see . . .
 If those remembered by you
are to think of you and not me,
 it seems to me that the memento
 or compliment you bestow
should have a name beginning with "V,"

such as Vera, El Greco's only
 daughter (though it has never been
proved that he had one), her starchy
 veil, inside chiffon; the stone in her
 ring, like her eyes; one hand on
her snow-leopard wrap, the fur widely

dotted with black. It could be a vignette—
 a replica, framed oval—
bordered by a vine or vinelet.
 Or give a mere flower, said to mean the
 love of truth or truth of
love—in other words, a violet.

Verse—unabashedly bold—is appropriate;
 and always it should be as neat
as the most careful writer's "8."
 Any valentine that is *written*
Is as the *vendange* to the vine.
 Might verse not best confuse itself with fate?

SUN

Hope and Fear accost him

       "No man may him hyde
       From Deth holow-eyed";
  For us, this inconvenient truth does not suffice.
   You are not male or female, but a plan
   deep-set within the heart of man.
Splendid with splendor hid you come, from your Arab abode,
a fiery topaz smothered in the hand of a great prince who rode
    before you, Sun—whom you outran,
    piercing his caravan.

      O Sun, you shall stay
      with us; holiday,
   consuming wrath, be wound in a device
  of Moorish gorgeousness, round glasses spun
  to flame as hemispheres of one
great hour-glass dwindling to a stem. Consume hostility;
employ your weapon in this meeting-place of surging enmity!
    Insurgent feet shall not outrun
    multiplied flames, O Sun.

HITHERTO UNCOLLECTED

"AVEC ARDEUR"

Dear Ezra, who knows what cadence is.

I've been thinking—mean, cogitating:

Make a fuss
and be tedious.

I'm annoyed?
Yes; am. I avoid

"adore"
and "bore";

am, I
say, by

the word
(bore) bored.

I refuse
to use

"divine"
to mean

something
pleasing:

"terrific color"
for some horror.

Though flat
myself, I'd say that

"Atlas"
(pressed glass)

looks best
embossed.

I refuse
to use

"enchant,"
"dement";

even "fright-
ful plight"
(however justified)

or "frivol-
ous fool"
(however suitable).

I've escaped?
am still trapped

by these
word diseases.

Without pauses,
the phrases

lack lyric
force, unlike

Attic
Alcaic,

or freak
calico-Greek.

This is not verse
of course.

I'm sure of this;

Nothing mundane is divine;
Nothing divine is mundane.

LOVE IN AMERICA—

Whatever it is, it's a passion—
a benign dementia that should be
engulfing America, fed in a way
    the opposite of the way
in which the Minotaur was fed.
It's a Midas of tenderness;
    from the heart;
nothing else. From one with ability
to bear being misunderstood—
    take the blame, with "nobility
    that is action," identifying itself with
    pioneer unperfunctoriness

    without brazenness or
    bigness of overgrown
    undergrown shallowness.

Whatever it is, let it be without
    affectation.

Yes, yes, yes, *yes*.

TIPPOO'S TIGER

The tiger was his prototype.
The forefeet of his throne were tiger's feet.
He mounted by a four-square pyramid of silver stairs converging
                                                    as they rose.

The jackets of his infantry and palace guard
bore little woven stripes incurved like buttonholes.

Beneath the throne an emerald carpet lay.
Approaching it, each subject kissed nine times
the carpet's velvet face of meadow-green.

Tipu owned sixteen hunting-cats to course the antelope
until his one great polecat ferret with exciting tail
escaped through its unlatched hut-door along a plank
above a ditch; paused, drank, and disappeared—
precursor of its master's fate.

His weapons were engraved with tiger claws and teeth
in spiral characters that said the conqueror is God.
The infidel claimed Tipu's helmet and cuirasse
and a vast toy, a curious automaton—
a man killed by a tiger; with organ pipes inside
from which blood-curdling cries merged with inhuman groans.
The tiger moved its tail as the man moved his arm.

This ballad still awaits a tiger-hearted bard.
    Great losses for the enemy
can't make the owner's loss less hard.

THE CAMPERDOWN ELM

Gift of Mr. A. G. Burgess to Prospect Park, Brooklyn, 1872.

I think, in connection with this weeping elm,
of "Kindred Spirits" at the edge of a rockledge
           overlooking a stream:
Thanatopsis-invoking tree-loving Bryant
conversing with Thomas Cole
in Asher Durand's painting of them
under the filigree of an elm overhead.

No doubt they had seen other trees—lindens,
maples and sycamores, oaks and the Paris
street-tree, the horse-chestnut; but imagine
their rapture, had they come on the Camperdown elm's
massiveness and "the intricate pattern of its branches,"
arching high, curving low, in its mist of fine twigs.
The Bartlett tree-cavity specialist saw it
and thrust his arm the whole length of the hollowness
of its torso and there were six small cavities also.

Props are needed and tree-food. It is still leafing;
still there. *Mortal* though. We must save it. It is
           our crowning curio.

MERCIFULLY

I am hard to disgust,
but a pretentious poet can do it;
a person without a tap root; and
impercipience can do it; did it.

But why talk about it—
offset by Musica Antiqua's
"Legendary Performance"
of impassioned exactitude.

An elate tongue is music. . . . .
the plain truth—complex truth—
in which unnatural emphases,
"passi - on" and "divis - i-on,"
sound natural. Play it all; *do;*
except in uproars of conversation.

Celestial refrain. . . . . My mind
hears it again. Without music
life is flat—bare existence.
Dirgelike David and Absalom. That.
                    Let it be that.

"REMINISCENT OF A WAVE AT THE CURL"

On a kind of Christmas Day—
big flakes blurring everything—
cat-power matching momentum,
each kitten having capsized the other,
   one kitten fell;
the other's hind leg planted hard
on the eye that had guided the onslaught—
ears laid back, both tails lashing—
a cynic might have said,
"Sir Francis Bacon defined it:
'Foreign war is like the heat of exercise;
civil war is like the heat of a fever.' "

Not at all. The expert would say,
   "Rather hard on the fur."

ENOUGH

1969

Am I a fanatic? The opposite.
     And where would I like to be?
     Sitting under Plato's olive tree
or propped against its thick old trunk,

          away from controversy
          or anyone choleric.

If you would see stones set right, unthreatened
     by mortar (masons say "mud"),
     squared and smooth, let them rise as they should,
Ben Jonson said, or he implied.

          In "Discoveries" he then said,
          "Stand for truth. It's enough."

THE MAGICIAN'S RETREAT

of moderate height,
(I have seen it)
cloudy but bright inside
like a moonstone,
while a yellow glow
from a shutter-crack shone,
and a blue glow from the lamppost
close to the front door.
It left nothing of which to complain,
nothing more to obtain,
consummately plain.

A blacl: tree mass rose at the back
almost touching the eaves
with the definiteness of Magritte,
was above all discreet.

PREVALENT AT ONE TIME

I've always wanted a gig
semi-circular like a fig
for a very fast horse with long tail
for one person, of course;

and then a tiger-skin rug,
for my Japanese pug,
the whole thing glossy black.
I'm no hypochondriac.

Selections from

THE FABLES OF
LA FONTAINE (1954)

THE FOX AND THE GRAPES

A fox of Gascon, though some say of Norman descent,
When starved till faint gazed up at a trellis to which grapes
                                         were tied—
          Matured till they glowed with a purplish tint
          As though there were gems inside.
Now grapes were what our adventurer on strained haunches
                                         chanced to crave
          But because he could not reach the vine
He said, "These grapes are sour; I'll leave them for some knave."

Better, I think, than an embittered whine.

(Book Three, XI)

THE LION IN LOVE

To Mademoiselle de Sévigné

Mademoiselle—goddess instead—
In whom the Graces find a school
Although you are more beautiful,
Even if with averted head,
Might you not be entertained
By a tale that is unadorned—
Hearing with no more than a quiver
Of a lion whom Love knew how to conquer.
Love is a curious mastery,
In name alone a felicity.
Better know of than know the thing.
If too personal and thus trespassing,
I'm saying what may seem to you an offense,
A fable could not offend your ear.
This one, assured of your lenience,
Attests its devotion embodied here,
And kneels in sworn obedience.

Before their speech was obstructed,
Lions or such as were attracted
To young girls, sought an alliance.
Why not? since as paragons of puissance,
They were at that time knightly fellows
Of mettle and intelligence
Adorned by manes like haloes.

The point of the preamble follows.
A lion—one in a multitude—
Met in a meadow as he fared,
A shepherdess for whom he cared.
He sought to win her if he could,

Though the father would have preferred
A less ferocious son-in-law.
To consent undoubtedly was hard;
Fear meant that the alternate was barred.
Moreover, refuse and he foresaw
That some fine day the two might explain
Clandestine marriage as the chain
That fettered the lass, bewitched beyond cure,
By fashions conducive to hauteur,
And a fancy that shaggy shoulder fur
Made her willful lover handsomer.
The father with despair choked down,
Said though at heart constrained to frown,
"The child is a dainty one; better wait;
You might let your claw points scratch her
When your heavy forepaws touch her.
You could if not too importunate,
Have your claws clipped. And there in front,
See that your teeth are filed blunt,
Because a kiss might be enjoyed
By you the more, I should think,
If my daughter were not forced to shrink
Because improvidently annoyed."
The enthralled animal mellowed,
His mind's eye having been shuttered.
Without teeth or claws it followed
That the fortress was shattered.
Dogs were loosed; defenses were gone:
The consequence was slight resistance.

Love, ah Love, when your slipknot's drawn,
One can but say, "Farewell, good sense."

(*Book Four, I*)

THE ANIMALS SICK OF THE PLAGUE

A malady smote the earth one year,
        Felling beasts and infecting all with fear,
To prove to them what grave offenders they were;
Although plague was the name by which it was known,
For it literally congested Acheron,
        Warring on creatures everywhere,
It did not bear off all but all were endangered.
        Any that lingered barely stirred—
Could merely breathe and that diseasedly.
        Nothing aroused their energy.
        Neither wolf nor fox disappeared
        To stalk young prey as it sunned.
        The demoralized doves scattered
        And love starved; life was moribund.

When the lion had called his constituency
        He said, "Dear friends, this is heaven's remedy
        For the sins we have thought a boon.
        So he who is guiltiest
Should sacrifice his good to that of the rest
And possibly most of us will then be immune.
In accord with the past, history suggests to one,
        Penance as atoning for evil done.
So without subterfuge, braving the consequence,
        Let each search his conscience.
As for me, I have preyed on flocks of sheep so often
        That I have become a glutton.
        Because they had wronged me? not once.
Moreover I would devour him when I mastered
                The shepherd.
Therefore let me be sacrificed in recompense,
But first make a clean breast, not just *I* say how I offend:
We must have justice and detect the trespass,

254)

Then rend the culprit's carcass."
The fox said, "Sire, you are too good to rend;
Your sense of honor is excessively nice.
Eat sheep, Sire! Poor dolts, their loss is no sacrifice.
A sinful king? Oh no. You prove when you devour
      The beasts that you thought them superior.
      As for the shepherd, one would swear
      That he went where he ought to go,
Having become to any of us, high or low,
      A monster none can endure."
When the fox said this, applause deafened the cur
      And no one dared to consider
A tiger, bear, or other beast of prominence
      Guilty of any offense.
In fact, quarrelers of evident spleen
Were canonized for their innocent mien.
When his turn came the ass said, "To take a backward glance,
      I recall passing clerical domain,
The herbs and grass and hunger close to sustenance.
      Fiend take me, how could I refrain?
I nipped off as much grass as would lie on my tongue;
So sinned, if what we say must be disinterested."
They made too much noise to hear what the donkey said.
A wolf pronounced the verdict, to which he clung,
Convinced they had found the animal they must kill—
The battered rapscallion who had made the world ill.
He deserved to be hung as an example.
Eat another's grass! What could be more horrible.
      Death, only death was suitable
For the criminal—inflicted at once by spite.
And so, as you are weak or are invincible,
The court says white is black or that black crimes are white.

(Book Seven, I)

THE BEAR AND THE GARDEN-LOVER

A bear with fur that appeared to have been licked backward
Wandered a forest once where he alone had a lair.
This new Bellerophon, hid by thorns which pointed outward,
Had become deranged. Minds suffer disrepair
When every thought for years has been turned inward.
We prize witty byplay and reserve is still better,
But too much of either and health has soon suffered.

      No animal sought out the bear
      In coverts at all times sequestered,
      Until he had grown embittered
And, wearying of mere fatuity,
By now was submerged in gloom continually.
      He had a neighbor rather near,
      Whose own existence had seemed drear;
Who loved a parterre of which flowers were the core,
      And the care of fruit even more.
But horticulturalists need, besides work that is pleasant,
      Some shrewd choice spirit present.
When flowers speak, it is as poetry gives leave
      Here in this book; and bound to grieve,
Since hedged by silent greenery to tend,
The gardener thought one sunny day he'd seek a friend.
      Nursing some thought of the kind,
      The bear sought a similar end
      And the pair just missed collision
      Where their paths came in conjunction.
Numb with fear, how ever get away or stay there?
Better be a Gascon and disguise despair
In such a plight, so the man did not hang back or cower.
      Lures are beyond a mere bear's power
And this one said, "Visit my lair." The man said, "Yonder bower,
Most noble one, is mine; what could be friendlier
Than to sit on tender grass and share such plain refreshment

As native products laced with milk? Since it's an embarrassment
To lack what lordly bears would have as daily fare,
Accept what is here." The bear appeared flattered.
Each found, as he went, a friend was what most mattered;
Before they'd neared the door, they were inseparable.

As confidant, a beast seems dull.
Best live alone if wit can't flow,
And the gardener found the bear's reserve a blow,
But conducive to work, without sounds to distract.
Having game to be dressed, the bear, as it puttered,
Diligently chased or slaughtered
Pests that filled the air, and swarmed, to be exact,
Round his all too weary friend who lay down sleepy—
Pests—well, flies, speaking unscientifically.
One time as the gardener had forgot himself in dream
And a single fly had his nose at its mercy,
The poor indignant bear who had fought it vainly,
Growled, "I'll crush that trespasser; I have evolved a scheme."
Killing flies was his chore, so as good as his word,
The bear hurled a cobble and made sure it was hurled hard,
Crushing a friend's head to rid him of a pest.
With bad logic, fair aim disgraces us the more;
He'd murdered someone dear, to guarantee his friend rest.

Intimates should be feared who lack perspicacity;
Choose wisdom, even in an enemy.

(Book Eight, X)

THE MOUSE METAMORPHOSED
INTO A MAID

A mouse fell from a screech-owl's beak—a thing that I can not
pretend
    To be Hindoo enough to have cared
To pick up. But a Brahmin, as I can well believe, straightened
    The fur which the beak had marred.
    Each country has the code it's preferred;
    Though some scorn a mouse's pain—
We are hard; whereas a Brahmin would as soon disdain
    A relative's. He feels that he submits to a fate
    That transforms one at death, to a worm
Or beast, and lends even kings a transition state—
A tenet it pleased Pythagoras to affirm,
Deduced from that system, of which he was a ponderer.
Based on the same belief, the Brahmin sought a sorcerer,
Eager to right what had been unfair and procured a key
To restore the mouse to her true identity.
    Well, there she was, a girl and real,
Of about fifteen, who was so irresistible
Priam's son would have toiled harder still to reward her
Than for Helen who threw the whole world in disorder.
The Brahmin said to her, marveling at the miracle,
    Charm so great that it scarcely seemed true—
"You have but to choose. Any suitor I know
    Contends for the honor of marrying you."
    —"In that case," she said, "the most powerful;
    I would choose the strongest I knew."
Kneeling, the Brahmin pled, "Sun, it shall be you.
    Be my heir; share my inheritance."
    —"No, a cloud intervening," it said,
"Would be stronger than I and I be discredited.
    Choose the cloud for her defense."
—"Very well," said the Brahmin to the cloud, sailing on,

"Were you meant for her?"—"Alas," it answered, "not the one.
The wind drives me from place to place; when whirled through
the void:
I might affront Boreas and be destroyed."
　　　　So the distracted Brahmin cried
　　　　To the wind he heard, "O Wind, abide.
　　　　Embrace my child in whom graces dwell."
Then Boreas blew hard, but met a mountainside.
　　　　Deterred lest interests coincide,
The ground demurred and sparred,"Scarcely suitable;
　　　　A rat might be incommoded
And weaken me by some tunnel he needed."
　　　　Rat! at the word, Love cast his spell
　　　　On an ear attuned. Wed? at last she knew.
　　　　A rat! a rat! Can names not do
　　　　Love service? Ah, you follow well:
　　　　Silence here between us two.

We retain the traits of the place from which we came. This tale
Bears me out; but a nearer view would seem good
Of what sophism never had quite understood:
We all love sun; yet more, what has a heart and will.
But affirm the premise? queer supposition
That when devoured by fleas, giants are outdone!
The rat would have had to transfer the maid in his care
　　　　And call a cat; the cat, a wolf-hound;
　　　　The hound, a wolf. Carried around
　　　　By a force that was circular,
Pilpay would bear the maid to the sun's infinitude
Where the sun would blaze in endless beatitude.
Well, return if we can, to metamorphosis;
The Brahmin's sorcerer, as bearing upon this,
Had not proved anything but man's foolhardihood,
In fact had shown that the Brahmin had been wrong
　　　　In supposing, and far too long,
That man and worms and mice have in unison

Sister souls of identical origin—
　　　　By birth equally exempt
　　　　From change, whose diverse physiques, you'll own,
　　　　Have gradually won
　　　　Reverence or contempt.
Explain how a lass so fair, incomparably made,
　　　　Could not earn for herself redress
And have married the sun. Fur tempted her caress.

　　　　Now mouse and girl—both have been well weighed
And we've found them, as we have compared their souls,
　　　　As far apart as opposite poles.
We are what we were at birth, and each trait has remained
In conformity with earth's and with heaven's logic:
　　　　Be the devil's tool, resort to black magic,
None can diverge from the ends which Heaven foreordained.

　　　　　　　　　　　　　　　　(Book Nine, VII)

Notes

A NOTE ON THE NOTES

A willingness to satisfy contradictory objections to one's manner of writing might turn one's work into the donkey that finally found itself being carried by its masters, since some readers suggest that quotation-marks are disruptive of pleasant progress; others, that notes to what should be complete are a pedantry or evidence of an insufficiently realized task. But since in anything I have written, there have been lines in which the chief interest is borrowed, and I have not yet been able to outgrow this hybrid method of composition, acknowledgements seem only honest. Perhaps those who are annoyed by provisos, detainments, and postscripts could be persuaded to take probity on faith and disregard the notes.

M. M.

A title becomes line 1 when part of the first sentence.

Selected Poems

THE JERBOA (*page 10*)

Line 4: *The Popes' colossal fir cone of bronze.* "Perforated with holes, it served as a fountain. Its inscription states, '*P. Cincius P. I. Salvius fecit.*' See Duff's *Freedom in the Early Roman Empire.*" *The Periodical*, February 1929 (Oxford University Press).

Line 52: *Stone locusts.* Toilet box dating from about the twenty-second Egyptian Dynasty. *Illustrated London News*, July 26, 1930.

Line 70: *The king's cane.* Descripton by J. D. S. Pendlebury, *Illustrated London News*, March 19, 1932.

Line 71: *Folding bedroom.* The portable bedchamber of Queen Hetepheres presented to her by her son, Cheops. Described by Dr. G. A. Reisner. *Illustrated London News*, May 7, 1932.

Line 90: "There are little rats called jerboas which run on long hind-legs as thin as a match. The forelimbs are mere tiny hands." Dr. R. L. Ditmars, *Strange Animals I Have Known* (New York: Harcourt, Brace, 1931), p. 274.

CAMELLIA SABINA (*page 16*)

The Abbé Berlèse, *Monographie du Genre Camellia* (H. Cousin).

Line 13: *The French are a cruel race*, etc. J. S. Watson, Jr., informal comment.

Line 32: Bordeaux merchants have spent a great deal of trouble. *Encyclopaedia Britannica*.

Line 36: *A food grape.* In Vol. 1, *The Epicure's Guide to France* (Thornton Butterworth), Curnonsky and Marcel Rouff quote Monselet: "Everywhere else you eat grapes which have ripened to make wine. In France you eat grapes which have ripened for the table. They are a product at once of nature and of art." The bunch "is covered and uncovered alternately, according to the intensity of the heat, to gild the grapes without scorching them. Those which refuse to ripen—and there are always some—are delicately removed with special scissors, as are also those which have been spoiled by the rain."

Line 39: *Wild parsnip.* Edward W. Nelson, "Smaller Mammals of North America," *National Geographic Magazine*, May 1918.

Lines 43–44: *Mouse with a grape.* Photograph by Spencer R. Atkinson, *National Geographic Magazine*, February 1932. "Carrying a baby in her mouth and a grape in her right forepaw, a round-tailed wood rat took this picture."

Line 49: *The wire cage.* Photograph by Alvin E. Worman of Attleboro, Massachusetts.

NO SWAN SO FINE (*page 19*)

A pair of Louis XV candelabra with Dresden figures of swans belonging to Lord Balfour.

Lines 1–2: "*There is no water so still as the dead fountains of Versailles.*" Percy Phillip, *New York Times Magazine*, May 10, 1931.

THE PLUMET BASILISK (*page 20*)
Basiliscus Americanus Gray.

In Costa Rica

Line 11: *Guatavita Lake.* Associated with the legend of El Dorado, the Gilded One. The king, painted with gums and powdered with gold-dust as symbolic of the sun, the supreme deity, was each year escorted by his nobles on a raft, to the center of the lake, in a ceremonial of tribute to the goddess of the lake. Here he washed off his golden coat by plunging into the water while those on the raft and on the shores chanted and threw offerings into the waters —emeralds or objects of gold, silver, or platinum. See A. Hyatt Verrill, *Lost Treasure* (Appleton-Century, 1930).

Lines 13–15: Frank Davis, "The Chinese Dragon," *Illustrated London News*, August 23, 1930: "He is the god of Rain, and the Ruler of Rivers, Lakes, and Seas. For six months of the year he hibernates in the depths of the sea, living in beautiful palaces. . . . We learn from a book of the T'ang Dynasty that 'it may cause itself to become visible or invisible at will, and it can become long or short, and coarse or fine, at its good pleasure.' " A dragon "is either born a dragon (and true dragons have nine sons) or becomes one by transformation." There is a "legend of the carp that try to climb a certain cataract in the western hills. Those that succeed become dragons."

The Malay Dragon

W. P. Pycraft, "The Malay Dragon and the 'Basilisks,'" *Illustrated London News*, February 6, 1932. The basilisk "will when alarmed drop to the water and scuttle along the surface on its hind legs. . . . An allied species (Deiropteryx) can not only run along the surface of the water, but can also dive to the bottom, and there find safety till danger is past."

The Tuatera

The tuatera or ngarara. In appearance a lizard—with characteristics of the tortoise; on the ribs, uncinate processes like a bird's; and crocodilian features—it is the only living representative of the order Rhynchocephalia. Shown by Captain Stanley Osborne in motion pictures. Cf. *Animals of New Zealand*, by F. W. Hutton and James Drummond (Christchurch, New Zealand: Whitcomb and Tombs, 1909).

In Costa Rica

Line 15: *A fox's bridge.* The south American vine suspension bridge.

Line 73: *A ten-ton chain.* A seven-hundred-foot chain of gold weighing more than ten tons was being brought from Cuzco, as part of the ransom for Atahualpa. When news of his murder reached those in command of the convoy, they ordered that the chain be hidden, and it has never been found. See A. Hyatt Verrill, *Lost Treasure*.

THE FRIGATE PELICAN (*page 25*)

Fregata aquila. The Frigate Pelican of Audubon.

Giant tame armadillo. Photograph and description by W. Stephen Thomas of New York.

Red-spotted orchids. The blood, supposedly, of natives slain by Pizarro.

Lines 37–39: "*If I do well, I am blessed. . . .*" Hindu saying.

NINE NECTARINES (*page 29*)

"The Chinese believe the oval peaches which are very red on one side, to be a symbol of long life. . . . According to the word of Chin-noug-king, the peach *Yu* prevents death. If it is not eaten in time, it at least preserves the body from decay until the end of the world." Alphonse de Candolle, *Origin of Cultivated Plants* (Appleton, 1886).

"Brown beaks and cheeks." Anderson Catalogue 2301, to Karl Freund collection sale, 1928.

New York Sun, July 2, 1932, *The World To-day*, by Edgar Snow, from Soochow, China. "An old gentleman of China, whom I met when I first came to this country, volunteered to name for me what he called the 'six certainties.' He said: 'You may be sure that the clearest jade comes from Yarkand, the prettiest flowers from Szechuen, the most fragile porcelain from Kingtehchen, the finest tea from Fukien, the sheerest silk from Hangchow, and the most beautiful women from Soochow.' "

Line 41: *Kylin* (or Chinese unicorn). Frank Davis, *Illustrated London News*, March 7, 1931. "It has the body of a stag, with a single horn, the tail of a cow, horse's hoofs, a yellow belly, and hair of five colours."

TO A PRIZE BIRD *(page 31)*

(Published in *Observations* [New York, Dial Press, 1924]; not included in *Collected Poems*.)

Bernard Shaw.

IN THIS AGE OF HARD TRYING . . . *(page 34)*

Lines 2–3: "*It is not the business of the gods to bake clay pots.*" Turgenev, *Fathers and Sons*.

POETRY *(page 36)*

Longer version:

I, too, dislike it: there are things that are important beyond all
this fiddle.

Reading it, however, with a perfect contempt for it, one
discovers in

it after all, a place for the genuine.
Hands that can grasp, eyes
that can dilate, hair that can rise
if it must, these things are important not because a

high-sounding interpretation can be put upon them but because
they are

useful. When they become so derivative as to become
                                    unintelligible,
the same thing may be said for all of us, that we
    do not admire what
    we cannot understand: the bat
        holding on upside down or in quest of something to

eat, elephants pushing, a wild horse taking a roll, a tireless wolf
                                    under
    a tree, the immovable critic twitching his skin like a horse that
                                    feels a flea, the base-
ball fan, the statistician—
    nor is it valid
        to discriminate against "business documents and

school-books"; all these phenomena are important. One must
                                    make a distinction
    however: when dragged into prominence by half poets, the
                                    result is not poetry,
nor till the poets among us can be
    "literalists of
        the imagination"—above
            insolence and triviality and can present

for inspection, "imaginary gardens with real toads in them,"
                                    shall we have
    it. In the meantime, if you demand on the one hand,
    the raw material of poetry in
        all its rawness and
        that which is on the other hand
            genuine, you are interested in poetry.

Diary of Tolstoy, p. 84: "Where the boundary between prose and
    poetry lies, I shall never be able to understand. The question is
    raised in manuals of style, yet the answer to it lies beyond me.
    Poetry is verse: prose is not verse. Or else poetry is everything
    with the exception of business documents and school books."
"Literalists of the imagination." Yeats, *Ideas of Good and Evil* (A. H.
    Bullen, 1903), p. 182. "The limitation of his view was from the

very intensity of his vision; he was a too literal realist of imagination, as others are of nature; and because he believed that the figures seen by the mind's eye, when exalted by inspiration, were 'eternal existences,' symbols of divine essences, he hated every grace of style that might obscure their lineaments."

PEDANTIC LITERALIST *(page 37)*
All excerpts from Richard Baxter, *The Saints' Everlasting Rest* (Lippincott).

IN THE DAYS OF PRISMATIC COLOR *(page 41)*
Lines 23–25: "Part of it was crawling," etc. Nestor. *Greek Anthology* (Loeb Classical Library), Vol. III, p. 129.

PETER *(page 43)*
Cat owned by Miss Magdalen Hueber and Miss Maria Weniger.

PICKING AND CHOOSING *(page 45)*
Line 13: "*Sad French greens.*" *Compleat Angler*.
Line 18: "*Top of a diligence.*" Preparatory schoolboy translating Caesar. Recollected by Dr. E. H. Kellogg.
Lines 25–26: "*A right good salvo of barks,*" "*strong wrinkles.*" Xenophon's *Cynegeticus*.

ENGLAND *(page 46)*
Line 9: "*Chrysalis of the nocturnal butterfly.*" Erté.
Lines 34–36: "I envy nobody," etc. *Compleat Angler*.

WHEN I BUY PICTURES *(page 48)*
Line 13: *Silver fence.* "A silver fence was erected by Constantine to enclose the grave of Adam." *Literary Digest*, January 5, 1918; descriptive paragraph with photograph.
Line 18: "*Lit by piercing glances . . .*" A. R. Gordon, *The Poets of the Old Testament* (Hodder and Stoughton, 1919).

THE LABORS OF HERCULES *(page 53)*
Line 4: "*Charming tadpole notes.*" *The London Spectator*.
Line 25: "*That the Negro is not brutal . . .*" Reverend J. W. Darr, in a sermon.

NEW YORK *(page 54)*

Line 4: *Fur trade.* In 1921 New York succeeded St. Louis as the center of the wholesale fur trade.

Line 8: *"As satin needlework . . ."* George Shiras, Third, *Forest and Stream*, March 1918; *The Literary Digest*, March 30, 1918. "About the middle of June 1916, a white fawn only a few days old was discovered in a thicket and brought to the hotel. Here, in the company of another fawn, it grew rapidly. During the earlier months this fawn had the usual row of white spots on back and sides, and although there was no difference between these and the body color, they were conspicuous in the same way that satin needlework in a single color may carry a varied pattern. . . ."

Lines 18–19: *If the fur is not finer.* Frank Alvah Parsons: *The Psychology of Dress* (Doubleday, 1920) quotes Isabella, Duchess of Gonzaga: "I wish black cloth even if it cost ten ducats a yard. If it is only as good as that which I see other people wear, I had rather be without it."

Line 25: *"Accessibility to experience."* Henry James.

PEOPLE'S SURROUNDINGS *(page 55)*

Line 4: *"Natural promptness."* Thomas Humphry Ward, ed., *English Poets*. Webbe—"a witty gentleman and the very chief of our late rhymers. Gifts of wit and natural promptness appear in him abundantly."

Line 15: 1420 pages. Advertisement, *New York Times*, June 13, 1921: "Paper—As Long as a Man, as Thin as a Hair. One of the Linden-meyr Lines was selected by Funk and Wagnalls Company, publishers of *The Literary Digest* and *The Standard Dictionary*, for their twelve-page pamphlet on India Paper. India Paper is so extremely thin that many grew fearful of the results when the unwieldy size, 45 × 65 inches, was mentioned. No mill ever made so large a sheet of India Paper; no printer ever attempted to handle it. But S. D. Warren Company produced the paper and Charles Francis Press printed it—printed it in two colors with perfect register. Warren's India is so thin that 1420 pages make only one inch."

Line 18: *Persian velvet.* Sixteenth-century specimen in the exhibition of Persian objects, Bush Terminal Building New York City, December 1919, under the auspices of the Persian Throne: "The design consists of single rose bushes in pearl white and pale black outline, posed on a field of light brown ivory so that the whole piece bears the likeness of the leopard's spots."

Line 31: *Municipal bat-roost.* In San Antonio, Texas, to combat mosquitoes.

Line 34: Bluebeard's limestone tower at St. Thomas, the Virgin Islands.

Line 42: "*Chessmen carved out of moonstones.*" Anatole France.

Line 53: "As an escalator cuts the nerve of progress."·Reverend J. W. Darr.

Lines 62–67: *Captains of armies* . . . Raphael: *Horary Astrology.*

SNAKES, MONGOOSES . . . *(page 58)*

Line 7: "*The slight snake* . . ." George Adam Smith, *Expositor's Bible* (1890).

NOVICES *(page 60)*

Line 5: "Is it the buyer or the seller who gives the money?" Anatole France, *Petit Pierre* (1918).

Line 9: "*Dracontine cockatrices* . . ." Southey, *The Young Dragon.*

Line 10: "Lit by half lights of more conscious art." A. R. Gordon, *The Poets of the Old Testament.*

Line 13: "The cypress too seems to strengthen the nerves of the brain." Landor, "Petrarca," in *Imaginary Conversations.*

Line 15: "The Chinese objects of art and porcelain dispersed by Messrs. Puttick and Simpson on the 18th had that tinge of sadness which a reflective mind always feels; it is so little and so much." Arthur Hadyn, *Illustrated London News*, February 26, 1921.

Line 23: "*The authors are wonderful people.*" Leigh Hunt's *Autobiography.*

Line 26: "*Much noble vagueness.*" James Harvey Robinson, *The Mind in the Making* (Harper, 1921).

Line 36: "*Split like a glass against a wall.*" The Decameron, "Freaks of Fortune."

Lines 37–39: "*Precipitate of dazzling impressions* . . ." A. R. Gordon.

Line 42: "*Fathomless suggestions of colour.*" P. T. Forsyth, *Christ on Parnassus* (Hodder and Stoughton).

Lines 44, 47, 48: "*Ocean of hurrying consonants,*" "*with foam on its barriers,*" "*crashing itself out.*" George Adam Smith, *Expositor's Bible* (1890).

Line 46: "*Flashing lances . . .*" "*molten fires . . .*" Leigh Hunt's *Auto-biography* (1850).

MARRIAGE *(page 62)*

Statements that took my fancy which I tried to arrange plausibly.

Lines 14–15: "*Of circular traditions . . .*" Francis Bacon.

Lines 25–28: *Write simultaneously.* "Miss A—— will write simul-taneously in three languages, English, German, and French, talking in the meantime. [She] takes advantage of her abilities in everyday life, writing her letters simultaneously with both hands; namely, the first, third, and fifth words with her left and the second, fourth, and sixth with her right hand. While generally writing outward, she is able as well to write inward with both hands." "Multiple Consciousness or Reflex Action of Unaccus-tomed Range," *Scientific American*, January 1922.

Line 42: "*See her, see her in this common world.*" "George Shock."

Lines 48–55: "*That strange paradise, unlike flesh, stones . . .*" Richard Baxter, *The Saints' Everlasting Rest.*

Lines 65–66: "We were puzzled and we were fascinated, as if by some-thing feline, by something colubrine." Philip Littell, reviewing Santayana's *Poems* in *The New Republic*, March 21, 1923.

Lines 83–84: "*Treading chasms . . .*" Hazlitt: "Essay on Burke's Style."

Lines 91–97: "*Past states . . .*" Richard Baxter.

Lines 101–102: "*He experiences a solemn joy.*" "*A Travers Champs,*" by Anatole France in *Filles et Garçons* (Hachette): "*Le petit Jean comprend qu'el est beau et cette idée le pénètre d'un respect profond de lui-même. . . . Il goûte une joie pieuse à se sentir devenu une idole.*"

Line 108: "*It clothes me with a shirt of fire.*" Hagop Boghossian in a poem, "The Nightingale."

Lines 109–113: "*He dares not clap his hands . . .*" Edward Thomas, *Feminine Influence on the Poets* (Martin Secker, 1910).

Lines 116–117, 121–123: "*Illusion of a fire . . .,*" "*as high as deep . . .*" Richard Baxter.

Line 125: "Marriage is a law, and the worst of all laws . . . a very trivial object indeed." Godwin.

Lines 146–152: "*For love that will gaze an eagle blind . . .*" Anthony Trollope, *Barchester Towers.*

Lines 159–161: "*No truth can be fully known . . .*" Robert of Sorbonne.

Lines 167–168: "*Darkeneth her countenance as a bear doth.*" Ecclesiasticus.

Line 175: "*Married people often look that way.*" C. Bertram Hartmann.

Lines 176–178: "Seldom and cold . . ." Richard Baxter.

Line 181: "Ahasuerus' *tête-à-tête* banquet." George Adam Smith, *Expositor's Bible*.

Line 183: "*Good monster, lead the way.*" *The Tempest*.

Lines 187–190: "*Four o'clock does not exist . . .*" Comtesse de Noailles, "Le Thé," *Femina*, December 1921. "*Dans leur impérieuse humilité elles jouent instinctivement leurs rôles sur le globe.*"

Lines 194–196: "*What monarch . . .*" From "The Rape of the Lock," a parody by Mary Frances Nearing, with suggestions by M. Moore.

Lines 198–199: "*The sound of the flute . . .*" A. Mitram Rihbany, *The Syrian Christ* (Houghton, Mifflin, 1916). Silence of women—"to an Oriental, this is as poetry set to music."

Lines 200–204: "*Men are monopolists . . .*" Miss M. Carey Thomas, Founder's address, Mount Holyoke, 1921: "Men practically reserve for themselves stately funerals, splendid monuments, memorial statues, membership in academies, medals, titles, honorary degrees, stars, garters, ribbons, buttons and other shining baubles, so valueless in themselves and yet so infinitely desirable because they are symbols of recognition by their fellow-craftsmen of difficult work well done."

Lines 207–208: "*The crumbs from a lion's meal . . .*": Amos iii, 12. Translation by George Adam Smith, *Expositor's Bible*.

Line 211: "*A wife is a coffin.*" Ezra Pound.

Line 223: "*Settle on my hand.*" Charles Reade, *Christie Johnston*.

Lines 232–233: "Asiatics have rights; Europeans have obligations." Edmund Burke.

Lines 252–253: "*Leaves her peaceful husband . . .*" Simone Puget, advertisement entitled "Change of Fashion," *English Review*, June 1914: "Thus proceed pretty dolls when they leave their old home to renovate their frame, and dear others who may abandon their peaceful husband only because they have seen enough of him."

Lines 256–258: "*Everything to do with love is mystery . . .*" F. C. Tilney, *Fables of La Fontaine*, "Love and Folly," Book XII, No. 14.

Lines 286–287: "*Liberty and Union . . .*" Daniel Webster (statue with inscription, Central Park, New York City).

AN OCTOPUS *(page 71)*

Quoted lines of which the source is not given are from Department of the Interior Rules and Regulations, *The National Parks Portfolio* (1922).

Line 6: *Glass that will bend.* Sir William Bell, of the British Institute of Patentees, has made a list of inventions which he says the world needs: glass that will bend; a smooth road surface that will not be slippery in wet weather; a furnace that will conserve ninety-five per cent of its heat; a process to make flannel unshrinkable; a noiseless aeroplane; a motor engine of one pound weight per horsepower; methods to reduce friction; a process to extract phosphorus from vulcanized india-rubber, so that it can be boiled up and used again; practical ways of utilizing the tides.

Line 9: "*Picking periwinkles.*" M. C. Carey, *London Graphic*, August 25, 1923.

Lines 11–12: "Spider fashion." W. P. Pycraft, *Illustrated London News*, June 28, 1924.

Lines 13–14, 178: "Ghostly pallor," "Creeping slowly . . ." Francis Ward, *Illustrated London News*, August 11, 1923.

Line 15: "*Magnitude of their root systems.*" John Muir.

Line 16: "*Creepy to behold.*" W. P. Pycraft, *Illustrated London News*, June 28, 1924.

Lines 18–19: "*Each like the shadow of the one beside it.*" Ruskin.

Lines 46, 53–54, 180, 184, 185: "*blue stone forests,*" "*bristling, puny, swearing men,*" "*tear the snow,*" "*flat on the ground,*" "*bent in a half circle.*" Clifton Johnson, *What to See in America* (Macmillan, 1919).

Lines 29, 62, 80, 112, 116, 195: "*Conformed to an edge,*" "*grottoes,*" "*two pairs of trousers.*" "My old packer, Bill Peyto . . . would give one or two nervous yanks at the fringe and tear off the longer pieces, so that his outer trousers disappeared day by day from below upwards. . . . (He usually wears two pairs of trousers)." "*Glass eyes,*" "*businessmen,*" "*with a sound like the crack of a rifle.*" W. D. Wilcox: *The Rockies of Canada* (Putnam, 1903).

Line 93: "*They make a nice appearance, don't they?*" Overheard at the circus.

Line 125: *"Menagerie of styles."* W. M., "The Mystery of an Adjective and of Evening Clothes," *London Graphic*, June 21, 1924.

Line 133: *"Rashness is rendered innocuous,"* *"So noble and so fair."* Cardinal Newman, *Historical Sketches*.

Lines 145–146, 148–152: *"Complexities . . .,"* *"an accident . . ."* Richard Baxter: *The Saints' Everlasting Rest*.

Line 155: "The Greeks were emotionally sensitive." W. D. Hyde, *The Five Great Philosophies* (Macmillan, 1911).

SEA UNICORNS AND LAND UNICORNS *(page 77)*

Line 3: *"Mighty monoceroses,"* etc. Spenser.

Lines 10–13: *"Disquiet shippers."* Violet A. Wilson, in *Queen Elizabeth's Maids of Honour* (Lane), quotes Olaus Magnus, *History of the Goths and Swedes*, with regard to the sea serpent; says of Cavendish as a voyager, "He sailed up the Thames in splendour, the sails of his ship being cloth of gold and his seamen clad in rich silks. Many were the curiosities which the explorers brought home as presents for the ladies. The Queen naturally had first choice and to her fell the unicorn's horn valued at a hundred thousand pounds, which became one of the treasures of Windsor."

Lines 20–22: Sir John Hawkins "affirmed the existence of land unicorns in the forests of Florida, and from their presence deduced abundance of lions because of the antipathy between the two animals, so that 'where the one is the other cannot be missing.' "

Line 26: *"In politics, in trade."* Henry James, *English Hours* (1905).

Lines 30–31: *"Polished garlands,"* *"myrtle rods."* J. A. Symonds.

Line 32: Apropos Queen Elizabeth's dresses, "cobwebs, and knotts and mulberries." "A petticoat embroidered all over slightly with snakes of Venice gold and silver and some O's. with a faire border embroidered like seas, cloudes, and rainbowes."

Line 41: *The long-tailed bear*. C. H. Prodgers in *Adventures in Bolivia* (Lane), p. 193, tells of a strange animal that he bought: "It was stuffed with long grass and cost me ten shillings, turning out eventually to be a bear with a tail. In his book on wild life, Rowland Ward says, 'Amongst the rarest animals is a bear with a tail; this animal is known to exist, is very rare, and only to be found in the forests of Ecuador,' and this was where the man who sold it to me said he got it."

Line 52: "*Agreeable terror*." "The lover of reading will derive agreeable terror from Sir Bertram and The Haunted Chamber." Leigh Hunt's *Autobiography*.

Lines 52, 80, 82: "*Moonbeam throat*," "*with pavon high*," "*upon her lap*." "Mediaeval," an anonymous poem in *Punch*, April 25, 1923.

Line 57: *An unmatched device*. Bulfinch's *Mythology*, under "Unicorn."

Line 65: Herodotus says of the phoenix, "I have not seen it myself except in a picture."

Line 66: "*Impossible to take alive*." Pliny.

Lines 69–70: "*As straight . . .*" Charles Cotton, "An Epitaph on M.H.":
As soft, and snowy, as that down
Adorns the Blow-ball's frizzled crown;
As straight and slender as the crest,
Or antlet of the one-beam'd beast.

THE MONKEY PUZZLE *(page 80)*

Line 9: The Chile pine (*Araucaria imbricata*). Arauco, a part of southern Chile.

Line 19: "*A certain proportion in the skeleton*." Lafcadio Hearn, *Talks to Writers* (Dodd, Mead).

INJUDICIOUS GARDENING *(page 81)*

Letters of Robert Browning and Elizabeth Barrett (Harper, 1899), Vol. I, p. 513: "The yellow rose? 'Infidelity,' says the dictionary of flowers." Vol. II, p. 38: "I planted a full dozen more rose-trees, all white—to take away the yellow-rose reproach!"

TO A SNAIL *(page 85)*

Line 1: "The very first grace of style is that which comes from compression." *Demetrius on Style*, translated by W. Hamilton Fyfe (Heinemann, 1932).

"NOTHING WILL CURE THE SICK LION . . ." *(page 86)*

Carlyle.

TO THE PEACOCK OF FRANCE *(page 87)*

Lines 1, 10: "*Taking charge*," "*anchorites*." Molière: *A Biography*, by H. C. Chatfield-Taylor (Chatto, 1907).

THE PAST IS THE PRESENT *(page 88)*

Lines 7-8: "*Hebrew poetry is prose with a sort of heightened conscious-
ness.*" Dr. E. H. Kellogg in Bible class, Presbyterian Church,
Carlisle, Pennsylvania.

"HE WROTE THE HISTORY BOOK" *(page 89)*

At the age of five or six, John Andrews, son of Dr. C. M. Andrews, said
when asked his name, "My name is John Andrews; my father
wrote the history book."

SOJOURN IN THE WHALE *(page 90)*

Lines 14-15: "Water in motion is far from level." *Literary Digest.*

SILENCE *(page 91)*

Lines 2-4: "My father used to say, 'Superior people never make long
visits. When I am visiting, I like to go about by myself. I never
had to be shown Longfellow's grave or the glass flowers at Har-
vard.'" Miss A. M. Homans.
Line 13: Edmund Burke, in *Burke's Life*, by Sir James Prior (1872).
" 'Throw yourself into a coach,' said he. 'Come down and make
my house your inn.'"

What Are Years

RIGORISTS *(page 96)*

Sheldon Jackson (1834-1909). Dr. Jackson felt that to feed the Eskimo
at government expense was not advisable, that whales having been
almost exterminated, the ocean could not be restocked as a river
can be with fish, and having prevailed on the government to
authorize the importing of reindeer from Siberia, he made an ex-
pedition during the summer of 1891, procured sixteen reindeer—
by barter—and later brought others. *Report on Introduction of
Domestic Reindeer into Alaska*, 1895; 1896; 1897; 1899, by
Sheldon Jackson, General Agent of Education in Alaska. U.S.
Education Bureau, Washington.

LIGHT IS SPEECH *(page 97)*

Lines 10-11: Creach'h d'Ouessant aeromaritime lighthouse, the first observable—as planned—by ships and planes approaching the Continent from North or South America.

Lines 14–15: "*A man already harmed.*" Jean Calas, unjustly accused of murdering his son, and put to death, March 9, 1762. In vindicating him and his household, Voltaire "*fut le premier qui s'éleva en sa faveur. Frappé de l'impossibilté du crime dont on accusait Calas le père, ce fut lûy qui engagea la veuve à venir demander justice au Roy....*" *The History of the Misfortunes of John Calas, a Victim to Fanaticism, to which is added a Letter from M. Calas to His Wife and Children; Written by M. De Voltaire.* Printed by P. Williamson. Edinburgh, MDCCLXXVI.

Line 17: Montaigne, captured by bandits and unexpectedly released, says, "I was told that I owed my deliverance to my bearing and the uncowed resoluteness of my speech, which showed that I was too good a fellow to hold up."

Line 20: Littré (1801–1881) devoted the years 1839–1862 to translating and editing Hippocrates.

Lines 30–31: Bartholdi's Liberty Enlightening the World.

Lines 33–35: "*Tell me the truth . . .*" Marshal Pétain.

Line 39: "*Animate whoever thinks of her.*" Janet Flanner, "Paradise Lost," *Decision*, January 1941.

HE "DIGESTETH HARDE YRON" *(page 99)*

"The estrich digesteth harde yron to preserve his health." Lyly's *Euphues.*

Line 5: *The large sparrow.* "Xenophon (Anabasis, I, 5, 2) reports many ostriches in the desert on the left . . . side of the middle Euphrates, on the way from North Syria to Babylonia." George Jennison, *Animals for Show and Pleasure in Ancient Rome.*

Lines 7, 17–18, 31: *A symbol of justice, men in ostrich-skins, Leda's egg,* and other allusions. Berthold Laufer, "Ostrich Egg-shell Cups from Mesopotamia," *The Open Court,* May 1926. "An ostrich plume symbolized truth and justice, and was the emblem of the goddess Ma-at, the patron saint of judges. Her head is adorned with an ostrich feather, her eyes are closed . . . as Justice is blindfolded."

Line 40: *Six hundred ostrich brains.* At a banquet given by Elagabalus. See above: *Animals for Show and Pleasure in Ancient Rome.*

Lines 43–44: *Egg-shell goblets*. E.g., the painted ostrich-egg cup mounted in silver gilt by Elias Geier of Leipzig about 1589. Edward Wenham, "Antiques in and about London," *New York Sun*, May 22, 1937.

Line 44: *Eight pairs of ostriches*. See above: *Animals for Show and Pleasure in Ancient Rome*.

Line 60: Sparrow-camel: στρουθιοκάμηλος.

THE STUDENT *(page 101)*

(Published in *What Are Years* [New York: Macmillan, 1941]; not included in *Collected Poems*.)

Line 1: "*In America . . .*" "*Les Ideals de l'Éducation Française*," lecture, December 3, 1931, by M. Auguste Desclos, Director-adjoint, Office National des Universités et Écoles Françaises de Paris.

Line 10: *The singing tree*. "Each leaf was a mouth, and every leaf joined in concert." *Arabian Nights*.

Lines 23–24: "*Science is never finished*." Albert Einstein to an American student, *New York Times*.

Line 25: *Jack Bookworm*: see Goldsmith's *The Double Transformation*.

Lines 33–34: *A variety of hero*. Emerson in *The American Scholar*: "There can be no scholar without the heroic mind"; "let him hold by himself; . . . patient of neglect, patient of reproach."

Lines 37–39: *Wolf's wool* . . . Edmund Burke, November 1781, in reply to Fox: "There is excellent wool on the back of a wolf and therefore he must be sheared. . . . But will he comply?"

Line 44: "*Gives his opinion . . .*" Henry McBride, *New York Sun*, December 12, 1931: "Dr. Valentiner . . . has the typical reserve of the student. He does not enjoy the active battle of opinion that invariably rages when a decision is announced that can be weighed in great sums of money. He gives his opinion firmly and rests upon that."

SMOOTH GNARLED CRAPE MYRTLE *(page 103)*

Lines 16–18: "Bulbul is a broadly generic term like sparrow, warbler, bunting. . . . The legendary nightingale of Persia is the white-eared bulbul, *Pycnotus leucotis*, richly garbed in black velvet, trimmed with brown, white, and saffron yellow; and it is a true bulbul; . . . Edward FitzGerald told what Omar meant: that the speech of man changes and coarsens, but the bulbul sings eternally in the 'high-piping Pehlevi,' the pure heroic Sanskrit of the ancient poets." J. I. Lawrence, *New York Sun*, June 23, 1934.

Lines 26–27: "Those who sleep in New York, but dream of London." Beau Nash, *The Playbill*, January 1935.

Lines 31–32: *"Joined in friendship, crowned by love."* Battersea box motto.

Lines 45–47: *"Without loneliness . . ."* Yoné Noguchi paraphrasing Saigyo, *The Spectator* (London), February 15, 1935.

Lines 49–51: "By Peace Plenty, by Wisdom Peace," framing horns of plenty and caduceus, above clasped hands, on the first-edition title page of Lodge's *Rosalynde*.

BIRD-WITTED (*page 105*)

Sir Francis Bacon: "If a boy be bird-witted."

VIRGINIA BRITANNIA (*page 107*)

Cf. *Travaile into Virginia Britannia* by William Strachey.

Line 12: *A great sinner.* Inscription in Jamestown churchyard: "Here lyeth the body of Robert Sherwood who was born in the Parish of Whitechapel near London, a great sinner who waits for a joyful resurrection."

Lines 16–17: *Werewocomoco.* Powhatan's capitol. Of the Indians of a confederacy of about thirty tribes of Algonquins occupying tide-water Virginia, Powhatan was war-chief or head werowance. He presented a deer-skin mantle—now in the Ashmolean—to Captain Newport when crowned by him and Captain John Smith.

Lines 18–19: Ostrich and horseshoe. As crest in Captain John Smith's coat of arms, the ostrich with a horseshoe in its beak—i.e., invincible digestion—reiterates the motto, *Vincere est vivere.*

Line 63: *"Strong sweet prison."* Of Middle Plantation—now Williamsburg.

Lines 108–110: The one-brick-thick wall designed by Jefferson on the grounds of the University of Virginia.

Lines 115–116: *Deer-fur crown.* "He [Arahatec] gave our Captaine his Crowne which was of Deare's hayre, Dyed redd." *Travels and Works of Captain John Smith, President of Virginia and Admiral of New England, 1580–1631*; with Introduction by A. G. Bradley. Arber's Reprints.

Line 132: *The lark.* The British Empire Naturalists' Association has found that the hedge-sparrow sings seven minutes earlier than the lark.

SPENSER'S IRELAND (*page 112*)

Lines 5, 7–8, 51, 63–64: "*Every name is a tune*," "*It is torture*," "*ancient jewelry*," "*Your trouble is their trouble.*" See "Ireland: The Rock Whence I Was Hewn" by Don Byrne, *National Geographic Magazine*, March 1927.

Lines 10–11: *Venus' mantle.* Footnote, *Castle Rackrent*: "The cloak, or mantle, as described by Thady is of high antiquity. See Spenser's 'View of the State of Ireland.'"

Line 12: *The sleeves.* In Maria Edgeworth's *Castle Rackrent*, as edited by Professor Morley, Thady Quirk says, "I wear a long great-coat . . . ; it holds on by a single button round my neck, cloak fashion."

Line 39: "The sad-yellow-fly, made with the buzzard's wing" and "the shell-fly, for the middle of July." Maria Edgeworth, *The Absentee.*

Lines 53, 56: "*The guillemot.*" "*The linnet.*" Denis O'Sullivan, *Happy Memories of Glengarry.*

Line 58: *Earl Gerald.* From a lecture by Padraic Colum.

FOUR QUARTZ CRYSTAL CLOCKS (*page 115*)

Bell leaflet, 1939, "'The World's Most Accurate Clocks.' In the Bell Telephone Laboratories in New York, in a 'time vault' whose temperature is maintained within 1/100 of a degree, at 41° centigrade, are the most accurate clocks in the world—the four quartz crystal clocks. . . . When properly cut and inserted in a suitable circuit, they will control the rate of electric vibration to an accuracy of one part in a million. . . . When you call MEridian 7–1212 for correct time you get it every 15 seconds."

Line 13–16: "*Appeler à l'aide d'un camouflage ces instruments faits pour la vérité qui sont la radio, le cinéma, la presse?*" "*J'ai traversé voilà un an des pays arabes où l'on ignorait encore que Napoléon était mort.*" Jean Giraudoux, "*Une allocation radiodiffusée de M. Giraudoux aux Françaises à propos de Sainte Catherine,*" *Figaro,* November 1939.

Line 45: *The cannibal Chronos.* Rhea, mother of Zeus, hid him from Chronos who "devoured all his children except Jupiter (air),

Neptune (water), and Pluto (the grave). These, Time cannot consume." Brewer's *Dictionary of Phrase and Fable* .

THE PANGOLIN (*page 117*)
Line 9: "*The closing ear-ridge*," and certain other detail, from "Pangolins" by Robert T. Hatt, *Natural History*, December 1935.
Lines 16–17: "*Stepping . . . peculiarly.*" See Lyddeker's *Royal Natural History*.
Lines 23–24: Thomas of Leighton Buzzard's vine: a fragment of ironwork in Westminster Abbey.
Lines 65–66: *A sailboat was the first machine.* See F. L. Morse, *Power: Its Application from the 17th Dynasty to the 20th Century*.

Nevertheless

ELEPHANTS (*page 128*)
Data utilized in these stanzas, from a lecture-film entitled *Ceylon, the Wondrous Isle* by Charles Brooke Elliott. And Cicero, deploring the sacrifice of elephants in the Roman Games, said they "aroused both pity and a feeling that the elephant was somehow allied with man." George Jennison, *Animals for Show and Pleasure in Ancient Rome*, p. 52.

Collected Later

THE ICOSASPHERE (*page 143*)
The Mellon Institute is responsible for a steel globe of a design invented by J. O. Jackson, which "solves a problem which has long baffled draughtsmen and engineers. Anybody who has tried to wrap a rubber ball without wrinkling or waste . . . will understand the nature of the problem. Steel, like wrapping-paper, is delivered in rectangles. . . . Mr. Jackson discovered that Plexiglass . . . has the same plastic flow as steel and . . . will writhe back into its exact original shape if placed under proper heat. So he moulded a four-inch sphere out of flat Plexiglass, studied the pattern and worked out a design whereby 'twenty equilateral triangles—the greatest number of regular sides geometrically possible—could be grouped

into five parallelograms and cut from rectangular sheets with negligible scrap loss.' " Waldemar Kaemffert: "Economy in the Use of Steel," *New York Times*, February 5, 1950.

Lines 1–4: "*In Buckinghamshire hedgerows . . .*" Statement by E. McKnight Kauffer.

Line 7: *Someone's fortune.* The $30,000,000 snuff fortune of a Mrs. Henrietta Edwardina Schaefer Garrett, who died childless and without a will in 1930. "Orphan's Court, Philadelphia, has reviewed more than 25,990 claims for the fortune. . . . Three persons were reportedly slain in quarrels; ten went to jail for perjury. . . . A dozen or more were fined, six died and two killed themselves." *New York Times*, December 15, 1949.

"KEEPING THEIR WORLD LARGE" (*page 145*) The Reverend James Gordon Gilkey, and "All too literally, their flesh and their spirit are our shield." *New York Times*, June 7, 1944.

VORACITIES AND VERITIES . . . (*page 148*)
Line 2: "*Grass-lamp glow.*" V. Locke-Ellis.
Line 7: "The elephant's crooked trumpet doth write."

"*Elephants*
. . . Yea (if the Grecians doe not mis-recite)
With's crooked trumpet he doth sometimes write."

Du Bartas: "The Sixth Day of the First Weeke."
Dance Index–Ballet Caravan Inc.: *Clowns, Elephants, and Ballerinas*, June 1946.
Line 8: "To a tiger-book." *Man-Eaters of Kumaon* by Jim Corbett.
Line 12: *With love undying.* As the closing words of the sixth chapter of Ephesians, the phrase lingered in my mind. I wrote this piece, came upon Mr. V. Locke-Ellis's "grass-lamp glow," substituted it for my less good equivalent; upon rereading his poems later, I noticed the phrase "with love undying," used by him also.

PROPRIETY (*page 149*)
Line 16: Bach's *Solfeggietto.* Karl Philipp Emanuel's (C minor).

ARMOR'S UNDERMINING MODESTY (*page 151*)
Line 11: *Hacked things out with hairy paws.* "The very oldest relics of man's early ancestors are crudely chipped stone. He gripped them

in his hairy paw and used them to hammer and chop with."
Oscar Ogg, *The 26 Letters*, p. 6.

Line 13: *Arise for it is day*. Motto of The John Day Company.

Line 22: *The bock beer buck*. Poster unsigned, distributed by Eastern
Beverage Corporation, Hammonton, New Jersey.

Line 27: *Ducs*. "In England, in the Saxon times, the officers or com-
manders of armies, after the old Roman fashion, were called
dukes, without any addition, but after the Norman conquest, the
title was no longer used; till, in 1538, Edward III created his son,
who was first called the Black Prince, Duke of Cornwall. . . . After
Edward the Black Prince, more were made. . . . The Black Prince
was created by a wreath on his head, a ring on his finger, and a
silver rod." *The Book of the Ranks and Dignities of British Society*,
attributed to Charles Lamb (New York: Charles Scribner's Sons,
1924).

Like a Bulwark

APPARITION OF SPLENDOR *(page 158)*

Lines 16–17: "*Train supported by porcupines . . .*" Oliver Goldsmith
in one of his essays refers to "a blue fairy with a train eleven yards
long, supported by porcupines."

Line 21: "*With the forest for nurse*." "All over spines, with the forest
for nurse." "The Hedgehog, the Fox, and the Flies," Book Twelve,
Fable XIII, *The Fables of La Fontaine* (New York: The Viking
Press, 1954).

THEN THE ERMINE *(page 160)*

Line 2: ". . . *spotted*." Clitophon; "his device was the Ermion, with a
speech that signified, Rather dead than spotted." Sidney's *Arcadia*,
Book I, Chapter 17, paragraph 4. Cambridge Classics, Volume I,
1912; edited by Albert Feuillerat.

Line 12: *motto*. Motto of Henry, Duke of Beaufort: *Mutare vel timere
sperno*.

Line 18: *Lavater*. John Kaspar Lavater (1741–1801), a student of
physiography. His system includes morphological, anthropological,
anatomical, histrionical, and graphical studies. Kurt Seligmann,

The Mirror of Magic (New York: Pantheon Books, 1948, page 332).

TOM FOOL AT JAMAICA *(page 162)*

Line 6: *mule and jockey*. A mule and jockey by "Giulio Gomez 6 años" from a collection of drawings by Spanish school children. Solicited on behalf of a fund-raising committee for Republican Spain, sold by Lord and Taylor; given to me by Miss Louise Crane.

Lines 8–9: "*There is submerged magnificence . . .*" The Reverend David C. Shipley, July 20, 1952.

Line 9: *Sentir avec ardeur*. By Madame Boufflers—Marie-Françoise-Catherine de Beauvau, Marquise de Boufflers (1711–1786). See note by Dr. Achilles Fang, annotating Lu Chi's "Wên Fu" (A.D. 261–303)—his "Rhymeprose on Literature" ("rhymeprose" from "Reimprosa" of German medievalists): "As far as notes go, I am at one with a contemporary of Rousseau's: 'Il faut dire en deux mots / Ce qu'on veut dire'; . . . But I cannot claim 'J'ai réussi,' especially because I broke Mme. de Boufflers' injunction ('Il faut éviter l'emploi / Du moi, du moi.')." *Harvard Journal of Asiatic Studies*, Volume 14, Number 3, December 1951, page 529 (revised, *New Mexico Quarterly*, September 1952).

Air: *Sentir avec ardeur*

Il faut dire en deux mots
Ce qu'on veut dire;
Les longs propos
Sont sots.

Il faut savoir lire
Avant que d'écrire,
Et puis dire en deux mots
Ce qu'on veut dire.
Les longs propos
Sont sots.

Il ne faut pas toujours conter,
Citer,
Dater,
Mais écouter.
Il faut éviter l'emploi
Du moi, du moi,
Voici pourquoi:

Il est tyrannique,
Trop académique;
L'ennui, l'ennui
Marche avec lui.
Je me conduis toujours ainsi
Ici,
Aussi
J'ai réussi.

Il faut dire en deux mots
Ce qu'on veut dire;
Les longs propos
Sont sots.

Line 13: *Master Atkinson.* I opened *The New York Times* one morning
(March 3, 1952) and a column by Arthur Daley on Ted Atkinson
and Tom Fool took my fancy. Asked what he thought of Hill Gail,

Ted Atkinson said, "He's a real good horse, . . . real good," and paused a moment. "But I think he ranks only second to Tom Fool. . . . I prefer Tom Fool. . . . He makes a more sustained effort and makes it more often." Reminded that Citation could make eight or ten spurts in a race, "That's it," said Ted enthusiastically. "It's the mark of a champion to spurt 100 yards, settle back and spurt another 100 yards, giving that extra burst whenever needed. From what I've seen of Tom Fool, I'd call him a 'handy horse.' " He mentioned two others. "They had only one way of running. But Tom Fool. . . ." Then I saw a picture of Tom Fool (*New York Times*, April 1, 1952) with Ted Atkinson in the saddle and felt I must pay him a slight tribute; got on with it a little way, then realized that I had just received an award from Youth United for a Better Tomorrow and was worried indeed. I deplore gambling and had never seen a race. Then in the *Times* for July 24, 1952, I saw a column by Joseph C. Nichols about Frederic Capossela, the announcer at Belmont Park, who said when interviewed, "Nervous? No, I'm never nervous. . . . I'll tell you where it's tough. The straight-away at Belmont Park, where as many as twenty-eight horses run at you from a point three quarters of a mile away. I get 'em though, and why shouldn't I? I'm relaxed, I'm confident and I don't bet."

In the way of a sequel, "Money Isn't Everything" by Arthur Daley (*New York Times*, March 1, 1955): " 'There's a constant fascination to thoroughbreds,' said Ted, '. . . they're so much like people. . . . My first love was Red Hay . . . a stout-hearted little fellow . . . he always tried, always gave his best.' [Mr. Daley: 'The same description fits Atkinson.'] 'There was Devil Diver, . . . the mare Snow Goose. One of my big favorites . . . crazy to get going. . . . But once she swung into stride . . . you could ride her with shoe-laces for reins. . . . And there was Coaltown. . . . There were others of course, but I never met one who could compare with Tom Fool, my favorite of favorites. He had the most personality of all. . . . Just to look at him lit a spark. He had an intelligent head, an intelligent look and, best of all, was intelligent. He had soft eyes, a wide brow and—gee, I'm sounding like a lovesick boy. But I think he had the handsomest face of any horse I ever had anything to do with. He was a great horse but I was fond of him not so much for what he achieved as for what he was.' With that the sprightly Master Theodore fastened the number plate on his right shoulder and headed for the paddock."

Lines 14–15: "*Chance is a regrettable impurity*." The *I Ching* or *Book of Changes*, translated by Richard Wilhelm and Cary Baynes, Bollingen Series XIX (New York: Pantheon Books, 1950).

Line 29: *Fats Waller*. Thomas Waller, "a protean jazz figure," died in 1943. See *The New York Times*, article and Richard Tucker (Pix) photograph, March 16, 1952.

Line 31: *Ozzie Smith*. Osborne Smith, a Negro chanter and drummer who improvised the music for Ian Hugo's *Ai-Yé*.

Line 31: *Eubie Blake*. The Negro pianist in *Shuffle Along*.

THE WEB ONE WEAVES OF ITALY *(page 164)*

Stanzas 1 and 2 mainly quotation from "Festivals and Fairs for the Tourist in Italy" by Mitchell Goodman, *New York Times*, April 18, 1954.

Line 12: "*Fount by which enchanting gems are spilt*." "The Monkey and the Leopard," Book Nine, Fable III, *The Fables of La Fontaine* (The Viking Press, 1954).

THE STAFF OF AESCULAPIUS *(page 165)*

Dr. Grace of Grace's Clinic, Brooklyn, deplores the need for hospitals and says that I imply it, but the intervention of hospital service for myself and others I cherish, in need of trained skill, apologizes for my allegiance.

Line 11: *Time*, March 29, 1954, article on the Salk vaccine.

Lines 17–20: *Selective injury to cancer cells* . . . Sloan-Kettering Institute for Cancer Research, *Progress Report VII*, June 1954; pp. 20–21.

Lines 22–25: *To sponge implanted* . . . Abbott Laboratories, "Plastic Sponge Implants in Surgery," *What's New*, Number 186, Christmas 1954.

THE SYCAMORE *(page 167)*

Lines 15–16: *Nine she-camel-hairs*. Imami, the Iranian miniaturist, draws "with a brush made of nine hairs from a newborn she camel and a pencil sharpened to a needle point. . . . He was decorated twice by the late Riza Shah; once for his miniatures and once for his rugs." *New York Times*, March 5, 1954.

ROSEMARY (*page 168*)

Line 17: "*Hath a dumb language.*" Sir Thomas More.

According to a Spanish legend, rosemary flowers—originally white— turned blue when the Virgin threw her cloak over a rosemary bush, while resting on the flight into Egypt. There is in Trinity College Library, Cambridge, a manuscript sent to Queen Philippa of Hainault by her mother, written by "a clerk of the school of Salerno" and translated by "danyel bain." The manuscript is devoted entirely to the virtues of rosemary, which, we are told, never grows higher than the height of Christ; after thirty-three years the plant increases in breadth but not in height. See "Rosemary of Plesant Savour," by Eleanour Sinclair Rohde, *The Spectator*, July 7, 1930.

STYLE (*page 169*)

Line 8: *Dick Button.* See photograph, *New York Times*, January 2, 1956.

Line 10: *Etchebaster.* Pierre Etchebaster, a machine-gunner in the First World War; champion of France in chistera (jai alai), pala, and mainnues. He took up court tennis in 1922, won the American championship in 1928, and retired in 1954. (*New York Times*, February 13, 1954 and February 24, 1955.) *New York Times*, January 19, 1956: "Pierre Etchebaster, retired world champion, and Frederick S. Moseley won the pro-amateur handicap court tennis tournament at the Racquet and Tennis Club yesterday. . . . The score was 5–6, 6–5, 6–5. Moseley, president of the club, scored the last point of the match with a railroad ace. Johnson and McClintock had pulled up from 3–5 to 5–all in this final set."

Line 10: *Soledad.* Danced in America, 1950–1951.

Line 27: *Rosario's.* Rosario Escudero, one of the company of Vicente Escudero, but not related to him.

LOGIC AND "THE MAGIC FLUTE" (*page 171*)

The Magic Flute. Colorcast by NBC Opera Theater, January 15, 1956.

Line 11: *Precious wentletrap. n.* [D. *wenteltrap* a winding staircase; cf.

G. *wendeltreppe*.] The shell of *E. pretiosa*, of the genus *Epitonium*. —*Webster's New International Dictionary*.

Lines 23–24: "*What is love . . .*" *Demon in Love* by Horatio Colony (Cambridge, Massachusetts: Hampshire Press, 1955).

Line 25: *Banish sloth*. "Banish sloth; you have defeated Cupid's bow," Ovid, *Remedia Amoris*.

BLESSED IS THE MAN (*page 173*)

Lines 1–2: *Blessed is the man* . . . Psalm 1:1.

Line 4: "*Characteristically intemperate*." Campaign manager's evaluation of an attack on the Eisenhower Administration.

Line 5: "*Excuse, retreat . . .*" Charles Poore reviewing James B. Conant's *The Citadel of Learning* (New Haven: Yale University Press)—quoting Lincoln. *New York Times*, April 7, 1956.

Line 8: *Giorgione's self-portrait*. Reproduced in *Life*, October 24, 1955.

Lines 11–12: "*Diversity . . .*," "*Citadel . . .*" James B. Conant, *The Citadel of Learning*.

Line 13: "*Takes the risk . . .*" Louis Dudek: "poetry . . . must . . . take the risk of a decision"; "to say what we know, loud and clear—and if necessary ugly—that would be better than to say nothing with great skill." "The New Laocöon, *Origin*, Winter-Spring 1956.

Lines 14–15 "*Would . . .*" "President Eisenhower Vetoes Farm Compromise [Agricultural Act of 1956]," *New York Times*, April 17, 1956: "We would produce more of certain crops at a time when we need less of them. . . . If natural resources are squandered on crops that we cannot eat or sell, all Americans lose."

Line 16: *Ulysses' companions*. "The Companions of Ulysses," Book
   Twelve, Fable I, *The Fables of La Fontaine* (The Viking Press,
   1954).
Line 22: Mitin (From *la mite*, moth). Odorless, non-toxic product of
   Geigy Chemical Corporation research scientists (Swiss). *New York
   Times*, April 7, 1956.
Line 23: "Private lies . . ." See note for line 13.
Line 27: "*Things which do appear*." Hebrews 11:3.

O to Be a Dragon

O TO BE A DRAGON *(page 177)*

Dragon: see secondary symbols, Volume II of *The Tao of Painting*,
   translated and edited by Mai-mai Sze, Bollingen Series 49 (New
   York: Pantheon, 1956; Modern Library edition, p. 57).

Lines 1–2: Solomon's wish: "an understanding heart." I Kings 3:9.

VALUES IN USE *(page 181)*

Philip Rahv, July 30, 1956, at the Harvard Summer School Conference
   on the Little Magazine, Alston Burr Hall, Cambridge, Massa-
   chusetts, gave as the standard for stories accepted by the *Partisan
   Review* "maturity, plausibility, and the relevance of the point of
   view expressed." "A work of art must be appraised on its own
   ground; we produce values in the process of living, do not await
   their historic progress in history." See *Partisan Review*, Fall 1956.

HOMETOWN PIECE FOR MESSRS.
ALSTON AND REESE *(page 182)*

Messrs. Alston and Reese: Walter Alston, manager of the Brooklyn
   Dodgers; Harold (Peewee) Reese, captain of the Dodgers.

Line 1: "The millennium and pandemonium arrived at approximately
   the same time in the Brooklyn Dodgers' clubhouse at the Yankee
   Stadium yesterday." Roscoe McGowen, *New York Times*, October
   5, 1955.

Line 2: *Roy Campanella*. Photograph: "Moment of Victory," *New
   York Times*, October 5, 1955.

Line 4: *Buzzie Bavasi*. "The policemen understood they were to let the players in first, but Brooklyn officials—Walter O'Malley, Arthur (Red) Patterson, Buzzie Bavasi and Fresco Thompson—wanted the writers let in along with the players. This, they felt, was a different occasion and nobody should be barred." Roscoe McGowen, *New York Times*, October 5, 1955. E. J. Bavasi: Vice President of the Dodgers. William J. Briordy, "Campanella Gets Comeback Honors," *New York Times*, November 17, 1955.

Line 6: "*How did you feel . . .*" [Joe Collins to Johnny Podres]: " 'The secret of your success was the way you learned to control your change-up. . . .' 'I didn't use the change-up much in the seventh game of the world series,' said Johnny. 'The background was bad for it. So I used a fast ball that really had a hop on it.' . . . 'Hey, Johnny,' said Joe, 'how did you feel when Amoros made that catch?' 'I walked back to the mound,' said Podres, 'and I kept saying to myself, "everything keeps getting better and better." ' " Arthur Daley, "Sports of the Times: Just Listening," *New York Times*, January 17, 1956.

Line 10: "*Hope springs eternal . . .*" Roscoe McGowen, "Brooklyn against Milwaukee," *New York Times*, July 31, 1956.

Line 11: *8, Row 1*. The Dodgers' Sym-Phoney Band sits in Section 8, Row 1, Seats 1 to 7, conducted by Lou Soriano (who rose by way of the snare-drum). "The Sym-Phoney is busy rehearsing a special tune for the Brooklyn income tax collector: It's "All of Me—Why Not Take All of Me?" William R. Conklin, "Maestro Soriano at Baton for 18th Brooklyn Season," *New York Times*, August 12, 1956.

Line 16: "*Four hundred feet . . .*" "Gilliam opened the game with a push bunt for a hit, and with one out Duke Snider belted the ball more than 400 feet to the base of the right-center-field wall. Gilliam came home but had to return to base when the ball bounced high into the stands for a ground-rule double." Roscoe McGowen, "Dodgers against Pittsburgh." Duke Snider "hit twenty-three homers in Ebbets Field for four successive years." John Drebinger, *New York Times*, October 1, 1956.

Line 19: "*Stylish stout.*" [A catcher]: "He crouches in his wearying squat a couple of hundred times a day, twice that for double-headers." Arthur Daley, "At Long Last," *New York Times Magazine*, July 9, 1956.

Line 29: *Preacher Roe's number*. 28. Venerated left-handed pitcher for Brooklyn who won 22 games in the season of 1951.

Line 42: "He's a Jake of All Trades—Jake Pitler, the Dodgers' first-base coach and cheer-leader." Joseph Sheehan, *New York Times*, September 16, 1956, "Dodgers Will Have a Night for Jake"—an honor accepted two years ago "with conditions": that contributions be for Beth-El Hospital Samuel Strausberg Wing. Keepsake for the "Night": a replica of the plaque in the Jake Pitler Pediatric Playroom (for underprivileged children).

Line 44: *Don Demeter*. Center fielder, a newcomer from Fort Worth, Texas. "Sandy Amoros whacked an inside-the-park homer—the third of that sort for the Brooks this year—and Don Demeter, . . . hit his first major league homer, also his first hit, in the eighth inning." Roscoe McGowen, *New York Times*, September 20, 1956.

Lines 45–46: *Shutting them out* . . . Carl Erskine's no-hitter against the Giants at Ebbets Field, May 12, 1956. *New York Times*, May 27, 1956.

ENOUGH: JAMESTOWN, 1607–1957 *(page 185)*

On May 13, 1957—the 350th anniversary of the landing at Jamestown of the first permanent English settlers in North America—three United States Air Force super sabre jets flew non-stop from London to Virginia. They were the Discovery, the Godspeed, and the Susan Constant—christened respectively by Lady Churchill, by Mrs. Whitney (wife of Ambassador John Hay Whitney), and by Mrs. W. S. Morrison (wife of the speaker of the House of Commons). *New York Times*, May 12 and 13, 1957.

The colonists entered Chesapeake Bay, having left England on New Year's Day, almost four months before, "fell upon the earth, embraced it, clutched it to them, kissed it, and, with streaming eyes, gave thanks unto God . . ." Paul Green, "The Epic of Old Jamestown," *New York Times Magazine*, March 31, 1957.

Line 48: *If present faith mend partial proof*. Dr. Charles Peabody, chaplain at Yale, 1896, author of *Mornings in College Chapel*, said past gains are not gains unless we in the present complete them.

MELCHIOR VULPIUS *(page 188)*

"And not only is the great artist mysterious to us but is that to himself. The nature of the power he feels is unknown to him, and yet he has acquired it and succeeds in directing it."Arsène Alexander, *Malvina Hoffman—Critique and Catalogue* (Paris: J. E. Pouterman, 1930).

Line 11: *Mouse-skin-bellows'-breath.* "Bird in a Bush . . . The bird flies from stem to stem while he warbles. His lungs, as in all automatons, consist of tiny bellows constructed from mouse-skin." Daniel Alain, *Réalités*, April 1957, page 58.

NO BETTER THAN A "WITHERED DAFFODIL" *(page 189)*

Line 2: "Slow, Slow, fresh Fount" by Ben Jonson, from *Cynthia's Revels.*

Line 11: *A work of art.* Sir Isaac Oliver's miniature on ivory of Sir Philip Sidney. (Collection at Windsor.)

IN THE PUBLIC GARDEN *(page 190)*

Originally entitled "A Festival." Read at the Boston Arts Festival, June 15, 1958.

Lines 11–15: *Faneuil Hall . . .* "Atop Faneuil Hall, . . . marketplace hall off Dock Square, Boston, Laurie Young, Wakefield gold-leafer and steeple-jack, applies . . . finishing paint on the steeple rod after . . . gilding the dome and the renowned 204-year-old grasshopper. *Christian Science Monitor*, September 20, 1946.

Line 13: *Grasshopper.* "Deacon Shem Drowne's metal grasshopper, placed atop old Faneuil Hall by its creator in 1749, . . . still looks as if it could jump with the best of its kind . . . thought to be an exact copy of the vane on top of the Royal Exchange in London." *Christian Science Monitor*, February 16, 1950, quoting *Crafts of New England*, by Allen H. Eaton (New York: Harper, 1949).

Line 27: "*My work be praise . . .*" Psalm 23—traditional Southern tune, arranged by Virgil Thomson.

Line 38: "*Self-discipline.*" "President Eisenhower attributed to Clemenceau . . . the observation, 'Freedom is nothing . . . but the opportunity for self-discipline.' . . . 'And that means the work that you yourselves lay out for yourselves is worthwhile doing—doing without hope of reward.'" *New York Times*, May 6, 1958.

SAINT NICHOLAS *(page 196)*

Line 3: *A chameleon.* See photograph in *Life*, September 15, 1958, with a letter from Dr. Doris M. Cochran, curator of reptiles and amphibians, National Museum, Washington, D.C.

FOR FEBRUARY 14TH *(page 198)*
Line 2: "*Some interested law . . .*" From a poem to M. Moore by Marguerite Harris.

COMBAT CULTURAL *(page 199)*
Line 29: *Nan-ai-ans.* The Nanaians inhabit the frigid North of the Soviet Union.
Line 32: *One person.* Lev Golovanov: "Two Boys in a Fight." Staged by Igor Moiseyev, Moiseyev Dance Company, presented in New York, 1958, by Sol Hurok.

LEONARDO DA VINCI'S *(page 201)*
See *Time*, May 18, 1959, page 73: "Saint Jerome," unfinished sketch by Leonardo da Vinci, in the Vatican; and *The Belles Heures of Jean, Duke of Berry, Prince of France*, with an Introduction by James J. Rorimer (New York: Metropolitan Museum of Art, 1958).

Tell Me, Tell Me

GRANITE AND STEEL *(page 205)*
See *Brooklyn Bridge: Fact and Symbol* by Alan Trachtenberg (New York: Oxford University Press, 1965).
Line 7: *Caged Circe.* See Meyer Berger's story (retold in *Brooklyn Bridge: Fact and Symbol*) of a young reporter who in the 1870s was unaccountably drawn to climb one of the cables to the top of the bridge's Manhattan tower, became spellbound, couldn't come down, and cried for help; none came till morning.
Line 9: "*O catenary curve.*" The curve formed by a rope or cable hanging freely between two fixed points of support. "Engineering problems of the greatest strength, greatest economy, greatest safety . . . are all solved by the same curve," John Roebling said. (Trachtenberg, p. 69.)

IN LIEU OF THE LYRE *(page 206)*

Written in response to a request from Stuart Davis, president of the *Advocate*, for a poem.

Line 4: *Sentir avec ardeur*. By Madame Boufflers—Marie-Françoise-Catherine de Beauvau, Marquise de Boufflers (1711–1786). See note on pages 284–285.

Line 11: *Professor Levin*. Harry Levin, "A Note on Her French Aspect," p. 40, *Festschrift for Marianne Moore's Seventy-Seventh Birthday*, edited by T. Tambimuttu (1964).

Line 14: *Lowell House Press*. Referring to a Lowell House *separatum*: *Occasionem Cognosce* (1963).

Line 17: *Gratia sum*. Bewick tailpiece, "a trickle of water from a rock, underlined by a heart carved on the rock," p. 53, *Memoir of Thomas Bewick Written by Himself* (Centaur Classics).

Line 27: *A bridge. Brooklyn Bridge: Fact and Symbol*, by Alan Trachtenberg (1965).

THE MIND, INTRACTABLE THING *(page 208)*

Line 26: *The Mermaid of Zennor*. See "The Ballad of the Mermaid of Zennor," in *Affinities*, by Vernon Watkins (New York: New Directions, 1962).

DREAM *(page 209)*

Suggested by Jerome S. Shipman's comment in *Encounter*, July 1965.

OLD AMUSEMENT PARK *(page 210)*

Port Authority photograph given to me by Brendan Gill.

AN EXPEDIENT—LEONARDO DA VINCI'S—
AND A QUERY *(page 212)*

See Sir Kenneth Clark: *Leonardo da Vinci: An Account of His Development as an Artist*. "Continuous energy. If everything was continuous in movement it could not be controlled by mathematics in which Leonardo had placed his faith."

Lines 21–22: *Nature the test*. See Leonardo da Vinci's *Notebooks*, translated by Edward MacCurdy.

Lines 31–36: "*Sad*" . . . "*Tell me if anything at all has been done?*" Dr. Henry W. Noss, Associate Professor of History, New York University, quoting Leonardo da Vinci in a lecture.

W. S. LANDOR *(page 214)*

See introductory note by Havelock Ellis to Landor's *Imaginary Conversations*.

TO A GIRAFFE *(page 215)*

Ennis Rees summarizes the *Odyssey*, I feel, when he finds expressed in it the conditional nature of existence, the consolations of the metaphysical: the journey from sin to redemption.

ARTHUR MITCHELL *(page 220)*

Mr. Mitchell danced the role of Puck in Lincoln Kirstein's and George Balanchine's City Center production of *A Midsummer Night's Dream*.

RESCUE WITH YUL BRYNNER *(page 227)*

See *Bring Forth the Children* by Yul Brynner (New York: McGraw-Hill, 1960).

Line 30: *Symphonia Hungarica*. By Zoltán Kodály.

CARNEGIE HALL: RESCUED *(page 229)*

Lines 3–4: "*Saint Diogenes . . .*" "Talk of the Town," *The New Yorker*, April 9, 1960.

Lines 13–14: "*Palladian majesty*." Gilbert Millstein, *The New York Times Magazine*, May 22, 1960.

TELL ME, TELL ME *(page 231)*

Line 9: *Lord Nelson's revolving diamond rosette*. In the museum at Whitehall.

Lines 21–22: "The literal played in our education as small a part as it perhaps ever played in any and we wholesomely breathed inconsistency and ate and drank contradictions." Henry James, *Autobiography (A Small Boy and Others, Notes of a Son and Brother, The Middle Years)*, edited by F. W. Dupee (New York: Criterion, 1958).

Hitherto Uncollected

LOVE IN AMERICA— *(page 240)*

Line 5: The Minotaur demanded a virgin to devour once a year.

Line 6: Midas, who had the golden touch, was inconvenienced when eating or picking things up.

Lines 10–11: Unamuno said that what we need as a cure for unruly youth is "nobility that is action."

Lines 13–15: *without brazenness or bigness* . . . Winston Churchill: "Modesty becomes a man."

TIPPOO'S TIGER *(page 241)*

Derived from a Victoria and Albert Museum monograph, "Tippoo's Tiger," by Mildred Archer (London: Her Majesty's Stationery Office, 1959).

See Keats's *The Cap and Bells.*

"Tippoo" is the original form of the name used in the eighteenth century; "Tipu" is the accepted modern form.

Lines 17–20: *a vast toy, a curious automaton* . . . A mechanical tiger "captured by the British at Seringapatan in 1799, when Tipu Sultan, ruler of Mysore in Southern India, was defeated and killed." Mildred Archer.

Line 18: *Organ pipes.* Cf. "Technical Aspects of Tipu's Organ" by Henry Willis, Jr., in Mildred Archer's monograph.

MERCIFULLY *(page 243)*

Lines 6–8: *An Evening of Elizabethan Verse and Its Music* —W. H. Auden and the New York Pro Musica Antiqua; Noah Greenberg, Director. *Legendary Performances* (Odyssey 32160171).

"REMINISCENT OF A WAVE AT THE CURL" *(page 244)*

Kittens owned by Mr. and Mrs. Richard Thoma.

THE MAGICIAN'S RETREAT *(page 246)*

Drawing by Jean-Jacques Lequeu (1757–1825), *Arts Magazine*, December/January 1967–68.

Line 14: René Magritte, Domain of Lights, 1953–54. *New York Times Magazine*, January 19, 1969, page 69.

Selections from
The Fables of La Fontaine

THE LION IN LOVE *(page 246)*
Dedication: *Mademoiselle de Sévigné*. Later Mme. Grignan; daughter
    of Mme. de Sévigné. Many of Mme. de Sévigné's letters were
    addressed to her.

INDEX OF TITLES AND OPENING LINES

(*Titles are in italics*)

FOR THE BEST IN PAPERBACKS, LOOK FOR THE

In every corner of the world, on every subject under the sun, Penguin represents quality and variety—the very best in publishing today.

For complete information about books available from Penguin—including Penguin Classics, Penguin Compass, and Puffins—and how to order them, write to us at the appropriate address below. Please note that for copyright reasons the selection of books varies from country to country.

In the United States: Please write to *Penguin Group (USA), P.O. Box 12289 Dept. B, Newark, New Jersey 07101-5289* or call 1-800-788-6262.

In the United Kingdom: Please write to *Dept. EP, Penguin Books Ltd, Bath Road, Harmondsworth, West Drayton, Middlesex UB7 0DA.*

In Canada: Please write to *Penguin Books Canada Ltd, 10 Alcorn Avenue, Suite 300, Toronto, Ontario M4V 3B2.*

In Australia: Please write to *Penguin Books Australia Ltd, P.O. Box 257, Ringwood, Victoria 3134.*

In New Zealand: Please write to *Penguin Books (NZ) Ltd, Private Bag 102902, North Shore Mail Centre, Auckland 10.*

In India: Please write to *Penguin Books India Pvt Ltd, 11 Panchsheel Shopping Centre, Panchsheel Park, New Delhi 110 017.*

In the Netherlands: Please write to *Penguin Books Netherlands bv, Postbus 3507, NL-1001 AH Amsterdam.*

In Germany: Please write to *Penguin Books Deutschland GmbH, Metzlerstrasse 26, 60594 Frankfurt am Main.*

In Spain: Please write to *Penguin Books S. A., Bravo Murillo 19, 1° B, 28015 Madrid.*

In Italy: Please write to *Penguin Italia s.r.l., Via Benedetto Croce 2, 20094 Corsico, Milano.*

In France: Please write to *Penguin France, Le Carré Wilson, 62 rue Benjamin Baillaud, 31500 Toulouse.*

In Japan: Please write to *Penguin Books Japan Ltd, Kaneko Building, 2-3-25 Koraku, Bunkyo-Ku, Tokyo 112.*

In South Africa: Please write to *Penguin Books South Africa (Pty) Ltd, Private Bag X14, Parkview, 2122 Johannesburg.*